VIEWPOINTS®
SERIES

Coal

Other Books of Related Interest:

Opposing Viewpoints Series

Energy Alternatives

Offshore Drilling

Renewable Energy

At Issue Series

The Alaska Gas Pipeline

The Energy Crisis

Green Cities

Current Controversies Series

The Green Movement

Nuclear Energy

"Congress shall make no law ... abridging the freedom of speech, or of the press."

First Amendment to the US Constitution

The basic foundation of our democracy is the First Amendment guarantee of freedom of expression. The Opposing Viewpoints Series is dedicated to the concept of this basic freedom and the idea that it is more important to practice it than to enshrine it.

OPPOSING
VIEWPOINTS®
SERIES

❘ Coal

Roman Espejo, Book Editor

GREENHAVEN PRESS
A part of Gale, Cengage Learning

GALE
CENGAGE Learning™

Detroit • New York • San Francisco • New Haven, Conn • Waterville, Maine • London

GALE
CENGAGE Learning

Christine Nasso, *Publisher*
Elizabeth Des Chenes, *Managing Editor*

© 2011 Greenhaven Press, a part of Gale, Cengage Learning.

Gale and Greenhaven Press are registered trademarks used herein under license.

For more information, contact:
Greenhaven Press
27500 Drake Rd.
Farmington Hills, MI 48331-3535
Or you can visit our Internet site at gale.cengage.com

For product information and technology assistance, contact us at

Gale Customer Support, 1-800-877-4253
For permission to use material from this text or product, submit all requests online at
www.cengage.com/permissions

Further permissions questions can be emailed to permissionrequest@cengage.com

Articles in Greenhaven Press anthologies are often edited for length to meet page requirements. In addition, original titles of these works are changed to clearly present the main thesis and to explicitly indicate the author's opinion. Every effort is made to ensure that Greenhaven Press accurately reflects the original intent of the authors. Every effort has been made to trace the owners of copyrighted material.

Cover Image © Alex Masi/Corbis.

LIBRARY OF CONGRESS CATALOGING-IN-PUBLICATION DATA

Coal / Roman Espejo, book editor.
    p. cm. -- (Opposing viewpoints) Summary: "Coal : is coal the future of energy?; Is coal use justified?; Should coal use be phased out?; Is coal mining safe?"-- Provided by publisher.
    Includes bibliographical references and index.
    ISBN 978-0-7377-5715-6 (hardback) -- ISBN 978-0-7377-5716-3 (paperback)
    1. Coal--Environmental aspects--United States. 2. Clean coal technologies--United States. 3. Coal mines and mining--Safety measures--United States. I. Espejo, Roman, 1977-
    TD195.C58C595 2011
    622'.334--dc22
                                                                    2011005636

Printed in the United States of America
1 2 3 4 5 6 7 15 14 13 12 11

Contents

Why Consider Opposing Viewpoints?

> *"The only way in which a human being can make some approach to knowing the whole of a subject is by hearing what can be said about it by persons of every variety of opinion and studying all modes in which it can be looked at by every character of mind. No wise man ever acquired his wisdom in any mode but this."*
>
> John Stuart Mill

In our media-intensive culture it is not difficult to find differing opinions. Thousands of newspapers and magazines and dozens of radio and television talk shows resound with differing points of view. The difficulty lies in deciding which opinion to agree with and which "experts" seem the most credible. The more inundated we become with differing opinions and claims, the more essential it is to hone critical reading and thinking skills to evaluate these ideas. Opposing Viewpoints books address this problem directly by presenting stimulating debates that can be used to enhance and teach these skills. The varied opinions contained in each book examine many different aspects of a single issue. While examining these conveniently edited opposing views, readers can develop critical thinking skills such as the ability to compare and contrast authors' credibility, facts, argumentation styles, use of persuasive techniques, and other stylistic tools. In short, the Opposing Viewpoints Series is an ideal way to attain the higher-level thinking and reading skills so essential in a culture of diverse and contradictory opinions.

In addition to providing a tool for critical thinking, Opposing Viewpoints books challenge readers to question their own strongly held opinions and assumptions. Most people form their opinions on the basis of upbringing, peer pressure, and personal, cultural, or professional bias. By reading carefully balanced opposing views, readers must directly confront new ideas as well as the opinions of those with whom they disagree. This is not to simplistically argue that everyone who reads opposing views will—or should—change his or her opinion. Instead, the series enhances readers' understanding of their own views by encouraging confrontation with opposing ideas. Careful examination of others' views can lead to the readers' understanding of the logical inconsistencies in their own opinions, perspective on why they hold an opinion, and the consideration of the possibility that their opinion requires further evaluation.

Evaluating Other Opinions

To ensure that this type of examination occurs, Opposing Viewpoints books present all types of opinions. Prominent spokespeople on different sides of each issue as well as well-known professionals from many disciplines challenge the reader. An additional goal of the series is to provide a forum for other, less known, or even unpopular viewpoints. The opinion of an ordinary person who has had to make the decision to cut off life support from a terminally ill relative, for example, may be just as valuable and provide just as much insight as a medical ethicist's professional opinion. The editors have two additional purposes in including these less known views. One, the editors encourage readers to respect others' opinions—even when not enhanced by professional credibility. It is only by reading or listening to and objectively evaluating others' ideas that one can determine whether they are worthy of consideration. Two, the inclusion of such viewpoints encourages the important critical thinking skill of objectively evaluating an author's credentials and bias. This evaluation will illuminate an author's reasons for taking a particular stance on an issue and will aid in readers' evaluation of the author's ideas.

It is our hope that these books will give readers a deeper understanding of the issues debated and an appreciation of the complexity of even seemingly simple issues when good and honest people disagree. This awareness is particularly important in a democratic society such as ours in which people enter into public debate to determine the common good. Those with whom one disagrees should not be regarded as enemies but rather as people whose views deserve careful examination and may shed light on one's own.

Thomas Jefferson once said that "difference of opinion leads to inquiry, and inquiry to truth." Jefferson, a broadly educated man, argued that "if a nation expects to be ignorant and free . . . it expects what never was and never will be." As individuals and as a nation, it is imperative that we consider the opinions of others and examine them with skill and discernment. The Opposing Viewpoints Series is intended to help readers achieve this goal.

David L. Bender and Bruno Leone,
Founders

Introduction

"The more I dug, the more I could see that a rich, deep vein of coal runs through human history and underlies many of the hardest decisions our world faces now."

Barbara Freese,
Union of Concerned Scientists expert
and author of Coal: A Human History.

The use of coal in what is now the United States can be traced to A.D 1000. In the Southwest, the Hopi people cooked food, heated their homes, and baked clay pottery with coal, gathering about 450 pounds a day through strip and underground mining. "After the arrival of the Spaniards, the Hopi stopped using coal, possibly because by then the easily mined supply of coal had dwindled and because [missionaries] introduced carts and iron tools as well as draft animals,"[1] suggests late anthropologist Trudy Griffin-Pierce. In the early 1670s, Jacques Marquette, a French Jesuit missionary, and Louis Jolliet, a French Canadian explorer, discovered the combustible rock (*charbon de terra*, in their words) on the Illinois River. By the beginning of the 1700s, Huguenot (a French Protestant minority) settlers in present-day Richmond, Virginia, also found coal, as evidenced by several mines appearing near the Potomac River on a map from 1736.

America's coal mining industry began as the colonies flourished. "The first coal 'miners' in the American colonies were likely farmers who dug coal from beds exposed on the surface and sold it by the bushel,"[2] states the National Energy Tech-

---

1. Trudy Griffin-Pierce, *Native Peoples of the Southwest*. Albuquerque: University of New Mexico Press, 2000.
2. NETL, "Key Issues & Mandates: Secure & Reliable Energy Supplies—History of U.S. Coal Use," www.netl.doe.gov/KeyIssues/historyofcoaluse.html.

nology Laboratory (NETL). In 1748, coal-mining activity near Richmond, Virginia, was the first to be commercialized. During the Revolutionary War, the colonists used coal to manufacture artillery and other items. "Chesterfield County's coal pits supplied the cannon factory at Westham (near Richmond) with fuel that was used in making shot and shells for the Continental Army,"[3] notes historian Martha W. McCartney.

Turning the wheels of the Industrial Revolution, coal fueled the technologies and machines that changed everyday life and commerce in the era. In 1816, the first street lights in the United States powered by gas from coal illuminated the city of Baltimore, Maryland. Fourteen years later, the coal-powered Tom Thumb locomotive went into commercial production; its wood-burning predecessors were swiftly adapted to run on coal. In 1839, inventor William Otis introduced the steam shovel. A major advancement in surface coal mining, Otis's machine could dig about 13,400 cubic feet of earth a day.

In 1848, Schuylkill County, Pennsylvania, became the home of the nation's first coal miners' union. "Because of the limited quantities of anthracite, or hard, coal in the United States, virtual monopolies were established shortly, while the vast regions of bituminous fields made soft coal a highly competitive industry," writes Carroll Thompson in the journal *Current History*. Thompson continues, "Life in the mines is hard, the industry is a difficult, hazardous one, and the life of a coal miners' leader in many ways matches that of the men."[4] And the demand for coal grew, particularly during the Civil War. "The fuel needs of the federal army and navy, along with their military suppliers, promised a significant increase in the demand for coal," asserts Sean Patrick Adams, a history profes-

3. Martha W. McCartney, "Historical Overview of the Mid-Lothian Coal Mining Company Tract," December 1989, Mid-Lothian Mines Park website. www.midlomines.org/history.html.
4. Carroll Thompson, "Labor's Problem: Real Wages," *Current History*, January 1950, quoted in *Chicken Bones*. www.nathanielturner.com/laborsproblemrealwages3.htm.

sor at the University of Florida. He adds, "The demand for mineral fuel in the Confederacy led to changes in southern coalfields as well."[5]

Coke, a solid residue of bituminous coal, took the place of wood charcoal as the fuel of choice for furnaces in iron production by the mid-1870s. With the emergence of the American iron and steel industries, the production of coal tripled that decade and into the 1880s. "Pennsylvania's investment in anthracite iron paid dividends for the industrial economy of the state and proved that coal could be adapted to a number of industrial pursuits,"[6] asserts Adams. Moreover, the invention of the incandescent light bulb and pioneering developments in energy cemented its place in America. According to NETL, "The roots of today's primary use of coal—electric power generation—can be traced back to Thomas Edison."[7] In fact, Edison built the first successful coal-fired power station in Manhattan, New York, in 1882.

In 1900, coal production in the United States rose to 269 million tons; by 1961, it had become the leading fuel of electric-power plants. In the mid-1970s, the oil embargo by the Organization of Petroleum Exporting Countries (OPEC) against the United States for its military support of Israel created an energy crisis and sparked interest in converting coal into synthetic fuels to replace petroleum-based gasoline. Indeed, coal production has grown 95 percent since 1973, reaching a record-breaking 1.17 billion tons in 2008. Coal production dipped in 2009 to 1.07 billion tons and generated 44.6 percent of the total electric power output, 3.6 percent lower than the previous year. According to the Institute for Energy Research (IER), wind energy, hydroelectric power, and natural gas filled this market share. "The idea that wind energy has the potential to replace most of our coal-burning power today

5. Sean Patrick Adams, "The US Coal Industry in the Nineteenth Century," EH.net, February 4, 2010. http://eh.net/encyclopedia/article/adams.industry.coal.us.
6. Adams, "The US Coal Industry in the Nineteenth Century."
7. NETL, "Key Issues & Mandates."

is a very real possibility," proposes US secretary of the interior Ken Salazar. "It is not technology that is pie-in-the sky; it is here and now,"[8] he asserts. Nonetheless, others question whether windmills will ever have an edge over the black mineral. "The reality is that wind is a high-cost option; by its nature it is limited in the amount of generation it can provide, and mandating its use can actually cause an increase in overall emissions,"[9] contends the American Coal Council (ACC). The authors in this volume, *Opposing Viewpoints: Coal*, debate these and other coal-related issues in the following chapters: Is Coal the Future of Energy? Is Coal Use Justified? Should Coal Use Be Phased Out? and Is Coal Mining Safe? As the most abundant domestic fossil fuel, coal is a topic of robust discussion and debate about the energy needs of the nation now and in the future.

8. Quoted in Wayne Parry, "Offshore Wind Power Could Replace Most Coal Plants in US, says Salazar," *Huffington Post*, April 6, 2009. www.huffingtonpost.com/2009/04/06/offshore-wind-power-could_n_183593.html.
9. American Coal Council, "Coal Facts: Time to Clean Up the Confusion over Coal," 2010. www.americancoalcouncil.org.

OPPOSING
VIEWPOINTS®
SERIES

Is Coal the Future of Energy?

Chapter Preface

The world's proven reserves of coal stand at 826 billion tons, according to a 2010 report from BP, a multinational oil and gas company. The United States leads with 238.3 billion tons of coal, followed by Russia with 157 billion tons, China with 114.5 billion tons, and Australia with 76.2 billion tons. In addition, BP claims that the reserves-to-production (R/P) ratio, which factors the present rate of extraction, indicates these supplies will last 119 years. "Proved coal reserves are determined by the technical and economical feasibility of recovery and, as these are subject to a number of variables, R/P ratios are likely to vary year-on-year," states the World Coal Association. The association adds that BP also notes that "as reserve figures are provided by each country's relevant local authorities, there is no uniform method of assessment; therefore variations are expected."[1]

Such variations are up for debate; conflicting figures abound on how much coal is left to mine. In 2008, David Rutledge, chair of the Division of Engineering and Applied Science at the California Institute of Technology, purported that the world had 662 billion tons remaining, including already depleted reserves. "The record of geological estimates made by governments for their fossil fuel estimates is really horrible," Rutledge said at a press conference that year. "And the estimates tend to be quite high. They over-predict future coal production,"[2] he added. In 2010, a study led by Tad Patzek, chair of the Department of Petroleum and Geosystems Engineering at the University of Texas at Austin, concluded that US coal production may peak as soon as 2011. "We are

1. "Frequently Asked Questions," World Coal Association. www.worldcoal.org/resources/frequently-asked-questions/.
2. Quoted in Alexis Madrigal, "World Coal Reserves Could Be a Fraction of Previous Estimates," *Wired*, December 17, 2008. www.wired.com/wiredscience/2008/12/world-coal-rese/.

near or at the peak right now," Patzek contended. "The only estimate that's credible is what actually comes out of the mines and how you project that into the future."[3] Still, a 2007 analysis from the National Academy of Sciences projected that the nation has enough coal to last for more than a hundred years, with 1,500 billion tons that may be economically feasible to produce at a later time. "It is safe to conclude that the U.S. is not running out of reserves," insisted Raja Ramani, coauthor of the analysis and a mining engineer at the University of Pennsylvania. "I do not see 2011 as the peak year of coal production,"[4] Ramani maintained. In the following chapter, the authors present their predictions on the future of the mineral resource and its role in energy.

3. Quoted in Mason Inman, "Mining the Truth on Coal Supplies," National Geographic Daily News, September 8, 2010. http://news.nationalgeographic.com/news/2010/09/100908-energy-peak-coal/.
4. Quoted in Inman, "Mining the Truth on Coal Supplies."

> "Scientists, engineers, global businesses, and government organizations are working diligently to develop advanced coal technologies that provide reliable and eco-friendly answers to our energy future."

Clean Coal Will Be the Energy of the Future

National Energy Technology Laboratory

The National Energy Technology Laboratory (NETL) is a research and development facility operated by the US Department of Energy. NETL writes in this viewpoint that clean-coal technologies can reduce the environmental impacts of coal use and meet the nation's need for reliable energy. For instance, NETL proposes that integrated gasification combined-cycle (IGCC) power can convert coal into a gas and remove its impurities before combustion. Additionally, the retrofitting of coal-powered plants and other advances, NETL states, have cut pollutant emission levels by 30 to 95 percent. Investments in clean-coal technologies, overall, will have significant benefits for the economy, environment, and national security, the author maintains.

National Energy Technology Laboratory, "Clean Coal Demonstration and Deployment: A Vital Step on the Path to a Cleaner Energy Future," Copyright © 2011 U.S. Department of Energy. All rights reserved. Reproduced by permission.

As you read, consider the following questions:

1. How efficiently do today's technologies capture the pollutants in coal before they escape into the atmosphere, as stated by NETL?

2. What was achieved through the Power Plant Improvement Initiative, according to the author?

3. How does NETL portray the United States and its coal use?

Coal is one of America's most valuable resources. It is affordable, plentiful, and generates nearly half of the Nation's electricity. Coal or its by-products are also used for industrial heat, for steelmaking, and in the production of a variety of high-value products such as plastics, tar, synthetic fibers, fertilizers, and medicines.

To take advantage of coal as an energy resource while minimizing its environmental impact, scientists, engineers, global businesses, and government organizations are working diligently to develop advanced coal technologies that provide reliable and eco-friendly answers to our energy future. They are also taking the next vital step on the path to a cleaner energy future: demonstrating these technologies at full scale and providing incentives to encourage wide-scale deployment.

The National Energy Technology Laboratory (NETL) is at the center of U.S. efforts to develop, demonstrate, and deploy new, near-zero emissions coal power technologies. The laboratory has more than 20 years of experience delivering success through clean coal technology demonstration programs. In fact, today, 75 percent of domestic coal-fired power plants include technology with roots in NETL's clean coal demonstration program.

The Nature of Coal

Today's coal originated from the remains of trees, ferns, and other plants that lived 300–400 million years ago. As layers of soil and decomposing organic material were slowly compressed over the millennia, the carbon content fossilized to create this "rock that burns." Mixed with the carbon were various amounts of impurities, including sulfur, nitrogen, mercury, and other minerals. When coal is burned, these impurities can combine with water vapor to form acid rain or particulate matter. Burning coal also creates carbon dioxide (CO_2), one of several greenhouse gases that contribute to global climate change.

Prior to the 1970s, the use of coal contributed to the pollution of our Nation's land, air, and waterways. To solve this problem, in the 1970s and early 1980s, laboratories across the country began taking strides to develop technologies to reduce the environmental impact of using coal. Today, we have ways to capture the pollutants trapped in coal before they escape into the atmosphere. We have technologies that can filter out 99 percent of the particulate matter, remove more than 95 percent of acid rain pollutants, and reduce the release of CO_2 to near zero by using coal more efficiently and capturing and sequestering the CO_2 that is produced.

Advanced Coal Technologies

Advanced coal technologies can improve the environmental performance of coal and lower costs. However, for these innovations to be adopted and their benefits realized, they must first be demonstrated at commercial scale. Commercial-scale demonstrations and deployment incentives are a necessary and effective means to move advanced coal technologies with near-zero emissions from the research and development stage into the commercial marketplace.

The first U.S. program to demonstrate advanced coal technologies with this goal in mind was the Clean Coal Technology Demonstration Program (CCTDP), which was launched by the U.S. Department of Energy (DOE) Office of Fossil Energy in 1986 and managed by NETL. Originally intended as a response to concerns over acid rain—which is formed when sulfur oxides (SO_x) and nitrogen oxides (NO_x) combine with water and air particles—the first demonstration program focused on commercializing new, more efficient coal conversion systems and novel processes to help reduce emissions. The program was carried out through a series of five national competitions aimed at attracting promising technologies that were unproven commercially. Thirty-three projects were eventually completed, and a new era in clean coal technology began.

One technology to come out of the program was the world's first generation of integrated gasification combined-cycle (IGCC) power plants. This clean coal technology turns coal into a gas and then removes impurities from the coal gas before it is combusted. Of the five IGCC power plants in the world that operate at commercial scale, two are located in the United States: the Wabash River IGCC plant in West Terre Haute, Indiana, and Tampa Electric Co.'s Polk Power Station near Tampa, Florida. Both plants received funding from the CCTDP program.

Another technology developed under the first clean coal program was circulating fluidized bed combustion. This process can efficiently burn a wide range of fuels with reduced emissions. The CCTDP-funded JEA Circulating Fluidized Bed Combustion Demonstration Project in Jacksonville, Florida, was the first project to prove that the circulating fluidized bed process could be carried out on a large scale.

More than 20 technologies demonstrated in the original program achieved commercial success. These technologies have been used to retrofit three-quarters of today's coal-fired power plants. The most common are SO_x control systems, or "scrubbers," and technologies to lower NO_x emissions, but they also encompass advanced coal processing technologies, fluidized bed combustion, coal gasification, and industrial process technologies. Combined, these advances have allowed U.S. use of domestic coal to continue, while cutting pollutant emission levels 30–95 percent.

In 1999 and 2000, the United States faced a new energy challenge: U.S. consumers were confronted with blackouts and brownouts in major regions of the country. Congress responded by directing DOE to issue "a general request for proposals for the commercial-scale demonstration of technologies to assure the reliability of the nation's energy supply. . . ." DOE's answer: the Power Plant Improvement Initiative. Known as PPII, the initiative was a single solicitation to secure demonstrations that specifically addressed concerns of electric power reliability.

Nine years later, four PPII projects were successfully completed. The projects have improved plant efficiency, reduced emissions, and turned coal ash into useful building materials, along with using innovative approaches such as neural network artificial intelligent systems to optimize plant operations.

Today's Situation

As the 20th century drew to a close, so did our Nation's major battles with SO_x, NO_x, and acid rain. With the beginning of the 21st century, attention to the environmental concerns of coal utilization has shifted to the potential health impacts of trace mercury emissions, the aggravation of respiratory illness by microscopic particles, and the global climate-altering impact of greenhouse gases.

With coal likely to remain one of the Nation's lowest-cost electric power resources in the foreseeable future, even more advanced clean coal technologies are needed. The most recent demonstration program, the Clean Coal Power Initiative (CCPI), is helping the Nation successfully commercialize superior power systems that will attain near-zero emissions, produce clean fuels, effectively manage CO_2, and produce electricity at efficiencies nearly double that of today's technologies.

25

CCPI is a multi-year program that is being implemented through a series of competitive multi-award solicitations. In the first CCPI round, in 2002, the criteria for candidate projects were very broad. The solicitation was open to "any technology advancement related to coal-based power generation that results in efficiency, environmental, and economic improvement compared to currently available state-of-the-art alternatives."

The second CCPI solicitation encouraged proposals to demonstrate advances in coal gasification systems, technologies that permit improved management of carbon emissions, and advancements that reduce mercury along with other power plant emissions. Two of the selected projects involve IGCC systems based on prior CCTDP demonstrations, and a third project addresses mercury control.

Introduced in August 2008, the third CCPI round focuses specifically on technologies that manage greenhouse gas emissions. Projects will demonstrate the integration of technologies that capture and sequester at least 300,000 tons per year of CO_2 emissions while operating at a minimum CO_2 capture efficiency of 90 percent.

Another large-scale program that is expected to play a major role in advancing clean coal technologies is FutureGen 2.0. Announced in August 2010, DOE awarded approximately $1 billion for the repowering project and associated CO_2 storage network. The FutureGen 2.0 facility will feature advanced oxy-combustion technology, which burns coal with a mixture of oxygen and CO_2 instead of air to produce a concentrated CO_2 stream for safe, permanent, storage. In addition, the technology being evaluated in FutureGen 2.0 creates a near-zero emissions plant by eliminating almost all of the mercury, SO_x, NO_x, and particulate pollutants from plant emissions. NETL studies have identified oxy-combustion as a potential cost-effective approach for existing and new coal-fired facilities to capture CO_2 for geologic storage.

Renewables Are Not a Replacement

Despite the moniker, coal is not king—coal is a part of a really good army. With energy demand continuing to go up, we're going to need all of our available domestic energy resources to help meet that demand. That means that renewable energy has an important role to play in our energy portfolio.

However, in most cases renewables simply are not a suitable replacement for coal.

Electricity is produced in base-load power and peaking power. Baseload power is the energy necessary to keep the electricity grid energized and meet a constant demand. Peaking power is energy that comes on and off throughout the day, when electricity usage and energy demand goes up. Peaking power uses intermittent power resources like solar and wind that produce electricity only when there's sufficient direct sunlight or sufficient sustained wind speed. For baseload power, you must use so-called hard-path fuels such as coal, which can provide power 24 hours per day.

Technology is going to evolve, and coal is one of those unique bridge fuels that will take us to that next energy renaissance. As a matter of fact, coal may fuel the next energy renaissance.

American Coalition for Clean Coal Electricity.
www.americaspower.org.

The Next Step

Demonstration is a major facet of NETL efforts to expand clean coal technologies, but deployment activities also play a significant role. To encourage industry to use advanced technologies, NETL helps design and implement over $10 billion of deployment activities.

NETL serves as financial reviewer and technical consultant to the Internal Revenue Service (IRS) and the DOE Loan Guarantee Program Office (LGPO). With NETL's assistance, the IRS has distributed over $2 billion of tax credits for the deployment of clean coal technologies. NETL has been assisting the LPGO on soliciting and awarding $8 billion of loan guarantees for fossil fuel-related projects.

Developing and using clean coal technologies in the United States will improve the environment while helping to ensure the Nation's energy security. But to make an even greater impact the technologies need to be deployed internationally. NETL works with international partners to develop and demonstrate advanced technologies to improve the environmental performance of coal-based power generation for the benefit of us all. In addition to other international research activities, NETL has cooperative R&D [research and development] agreements in place with Australia, Brazil, China, Israel, South Korea, and Poland.

According to the International Energy Agency's World Energy Outlook 2010 report, world total energy demand from coal will increase by 59 percent from 2008 to 2035. These statistics show that the United States is simply part of a larger world population that is going to look to coal as an energy source for a long time to come. Because of this, NETL plays a key role in the international community, encouraging worldwide deployment of advanced coal technologies through cooperative R&D and outreach efforts with more than 40 countries.

What NETL Has Accomplished

From an investment of about $2 billion over more than 20 years, the estimated benefits from the demonstration of clean coal technologies range from $25 billion to more than $115 billion. The National Research Council has affirmed that the program's economic, environmental, and national security benefits far exceed program costs. Furthermore, industry estimates that future returns on investment in clean coal will amount to $100 billion by 2020 and $1,380 billion by 2050.

NETL's clean coal program has a broad scope, encompassing today's technologies and tomorrow's possibilities. By continuously setting and achieving higher goals and being aware of the needs of domestic and international stakeholders, NETL will continue to create innovative technologies to maximize the benefits of using coal, our Nation's most abundant energy resource.

| *"The "clean coal" bandwagon will almost certainly grind to a stop because it is simply too expensive to keep going."*

Clean Coal Should Not Be the Energy of the Future

Richard Heinberg

Richard Heinberg is a journalist, senior fellow-in-residence at the Post Carbon Institute, and author of Powerdown: Options and Actions for a Post-Carbon World. *In the following viewpoint, Heinberg declares that clean coal is a dead end. He maintains that coal supplies are vastly overestimated, and the United States cannot afford to invest billions in carbon capture and storage (CCS) and integrated gasification combined-cycle (IGCC) if it is to research and develop an alternative energy infrastructure. Instead, a feasible energy policy would emphasize conservation, advances in energy efficiency, and citizens' transition to low-consumption habits and expectations, Heinberg concludes.*

As you read, consider the following questions:

1. How does the author support his argument that coal reserves are shrinking faster than expected?

2. Why does clean coal come at an energy cost, in Heinberg's opinion?

3. How does Heinberg respond to the case for the partial deployment of clean-coal technologies?

Many energy experts, politicians on both sides of the aisle, and representatives of the coal industry agree on the need to spend billions to develop technologies to capture and store the carbon from burning coal, thus making coal "clean" from a climate standpoint. President [Barack] Obama has repeatedly endorsed the development of "clean coal," and in July [2009] Department of Energy Secretary Stephen Chu announced that $1 billion of stimulus package funds would go toward re-launching FutureGen, a stalled project intended to show how carbon dioxide can be captured on a large scale from coal-fired power plants. The Waxman-Markey climate bill earmarks another $60 billion for "clean coal" research and development.

The "clean coal" argument runs like this: America is brimming with cheap coal, which provides almost half our electricity and is the most carbon-intensive of the conventional fossil fuels. The nation will need an enormous amount of energy over the next few decades, but renewable sources just aren't ready to provide all—or even the bulk—of that energy. Meanwhile, preventing catastrophic climate change requires that we stop venting carbon dioxide into the atmosphere. It is possible to capture and store the CO_2 that would otherwise be emitted from burning coal, and elements of carbon capture and storage (CCS) technology are already in use on a small scale. Put all of these factors together and the case for government funding of research and development of "clean coal" seems strong.

However, several recent studies of US coal supplies suggest that much that we think we know about coal is wrong. If these studies are correct, the argument for investing in "clean coal" becomes tenuous on economic grounds alone. These studies call into question the one "fact" that both pro-coal and anti-coal lobbies have taken for granted: that the US has a virtually limitless supply of cheap coal.

How Much Coal?

Doubts were first raised in a book-length 2007 report by the National Academy of Sciences titled "Coal: Research and Development to Support National Energy Policy", which noted that "Present estimates of coal reserves are based upon methods that have not been reviewed or revised since—1974," and concluded that a newer and better assessment "may substantially reduce the number of years' supply."

Also in 2007, an energy analytics organization founded by a member of the German Parliament, Energy Watch Group, released a study of US and world coal supplies concluding that global coal production will reach a peak and begin to decline sometime around 2025, and that US coal production will peak only slightly later—perhaps by 2030 or 2035.

Last December [2008] the USGS [US Geological Survey] issued a report on the nation's largest and most productive coalfield, in Wyoming, finding that, at current prices, only about six percent of the coal can be profitably mined; if coal prices soared, then more of the coal would be recoverable—but then coal wouldn't be economically competitive with other energy sources.

On what do these studies base their pessimistic assessments of coal's future?

America's coal resources are indeed vast—none of the studies claims otherwise. However, during the past century, coal *reserves* (the portion of total coal resources that can be mined profitably with existing technologies) shrank much faster than could be accounted for by the depletion of those resources through mining. That is because geologists are doing a better job now of taking into account "restrictions" that make most coal impractical to mine—factors having to do with location, depth, seam thickness, and coal quality. In recent years, some nations have reduced their booked coal reserves by 90 percent or more on the basis of new, more realistic surveys. The National Academy of Sciences report mentioned above is essentially a plea for an updated US national survey, and it offers abundant reasons for thinking that such a survey would almost certainly reveal a much smaller reserve base than the one on which current supply forecasts are founded.

Moreover, when it comes to forecasting future coal supplies the official agencies seem to have been asking the wrong question, namely, "When will the nation run out of coal?" The customary answer is, "Not for a couple of hundred years or more"—which is a sufficiently long period for current energy planning. But more relevant questions are, "When will it no longer be possible to increase the rate at which coal is being extracted?", and "When will coal cease to be an economically competitive energy source?" These are addressed in the Energy Watch Group study, which reasons that, long before the nation runs out of coal, production will peak and start to decline due to the depletion of easily accessible, high-quality deposits. Already some of America's most important coal regions are long past their glory days, and recent field surveys by the USGS (including the one cited above) suggest that the capacities of even the most abundant coalfields in the nation have been over-estimated.

No Cheap Coal, No "Clean Coal"

How would the prospect for "peak coal" sometime in the next two or three decades impact the debate over the development of carbon capture and storage? As we are about to see, the enormous investments that will be required to make coal "clean" only make sense if coal continues to be abundant and cheap.

The basic elements of carbon capture and storage technology already exist. Capturing carbon is relatively easy in coal gasification (IGCC) power plants, and such plants have been shown to be technically feasible. In such plants, coal, air, and water are brought together under high pressure and temperature, yielding "syngas," a mixture of carbon monoxide and hydrogen (along with solid waste byproducts); the hydrogen can be burned to turn a turbine to produce electricity, while the carbon monoxide is transformed into carbon dioxide—which can then potentially be piped to an underground sequestration site for permanent storage. IGCC power plants are efficient, using about a third less coal to produce a similar amount of electricity, and can also capture other pollutants from coal. However, nearly all existing US coal power plants are of an older, simpler type in which coal is burned directly, so replacing these with expensive-to-build plants in which the coal is first gasified will itself require enormous investment and decades of work.

We also know how to store carbon: the petroleum services industry routinely injects CO_2 into old oil wells to make it easier to extract the remaining crude. But the quantities of carbon dioxide sequestered this way are trivial when compared with the amounts spewed from coal-burning power plants annually. Gathering and storing two or three billion tons of carbon each year from hundreds of geographically scattered coal power plants will require the construction of an enormous system of pipelines, compressors, and pumps. A 2007 MIT [Massachusetts Institute of Technology] study, "The Future of Coal", found that if just 60 percent of the CO_2 from US coal-fired power plants were to be captured and compressed to a liquid, its daily volume would equal the amount of oil Americans consume each day (about 20 million barrels). The study also concluded that a huge increase in investment in industrial-scale demonstration plants would be required now even to know in 10 or 15 years if the technology can work at a meaningful scale. All of this underscores the basic fact that carbon capture and storage is going to be very expensive—if it is even possible to accomplish on the scale that is being proposed.

Yet there is a subtler but possibly even more decisive price tag for "clean coal": the energy cost. According to the most recent estimate (from Harvard University's Belfer Center), at least 30 percent of the energy produced by burning coal will be needed to run the system for capturing, compressing, pumping, and burying CO_2. Therefore any efficiency benefit from gasifying coal at IGCC power plants would be canceled out.

But already the average quality of coal being mined is declining—that is, we get less energy for each ton of coal burned today than we did ten years ago. This is a natural consequence of the "low-hanging-fruit" principle of resource extraction, in which we tend to consume the highest-quality, most easily accessed resources first.

So as time goes on, the US will need to burn more coal, while the coal itself will be more scarce and costly. And the technology used will be far more expensive and complex, both to build and to operate, than the system of power plants we have today. Taken together, these factors read like a recipe for cost overruns and spiraling electricity rates.

How high could coal-based electricity prices go? During the period from 2006 to 2008, prices for some grades of US coal doubled. This year the economic crisis has lowered demand for electricity and thus for coal, and so prices have softened. However, recent experience shows that, even in the absence of serious shortages, coal prices are increasingly subject to dramatic swings. Thus, taking higher coal prices into account, it is reasonable to assume coal-based electricity costs two to five times current rates by 2030. The current average generation cost of coal electricity is from 2 to 5 cents per kilowatt-hour [kWh]; compare that to the current average

Huge Liabilities

In addition to being difficult and expensive, CCS [carbon capture storage] is potentially dangerous: In 1986, an eruption of CO_2 from a naturally occurring pocket under a Cameroon lake bed instantly suffocated nearly 1,800 people; leaks from an underground storage site could be likewise deadly. "That stuff is crazy," says Tyson Slocum, who heads Public Citizen's energy project. "Totally unproven. Stuffing hundreds of millions of tons of carbon dioxide into the ground—there are huge liabilities."

James Ridgeway,
Mother Jones, *May/June 2008.*

cost for wind electricity of 3.5 to 7 cents per kWh (not counting tax credits), or about 12 cents per kWh for solar thermal electricity, or 25 cents per kWh for solar photovoltaic electricity, and the vulnerability of coal's economic dominance becomes apparent.

Imagine a scenario in which the US goes ahead with the attempt to develop "clean coal" technologies. During the coming decade tens of billions of dollars (mostly from government) would likely need to be invested in research and the construction of demonstration projects. By 2020, the price of coal will already have begun to rise, as supply problems multiply, yet "clean coal" technology won't be ready to deploy widely (the most ambitious proposals don't see that happening until after 2025). Even if renewable energy doesn't get cheaper due to technological advances (and most analysts assume it will), at some point along this timeline the "clean coal" bandwagon will almost certainly grind to a stop because it is simply too expensive to keep going.

What, Then, Are the Options?

The most likely course for the Obama Administration and Congress is to continue developing "clean coal" based on current market conditions, and to change course only as market conditions evolve. The problem with doing so is that large infrastructure investments require long-range planning, and the success of those investments depends upon an accurate forecast of future resource prices and demand for product. Decisions made now on the basis of assumptions about future coal prices that are wildly wrong could waste enormous sums of money and foreclose opportunities to invest in ways that would leave society much better off two or three decades from now.

Some environmental organizations, such as Natural Resources Defense Council (NRDC) and Environmental Defense Fund (EDF), argue that the nation will almost certainly continue burning coal in any case, and since we cannot allow the resulting carbon dioxide to exacerbate climate change, "clean coal" technology is worth the investment.

But what sort of energy policy could force "clean coal" into existence? Government could legislate that all new coal power plants must capture and store carbon. But then, for reasons already explained, few new plants would probably get built—other than demonstration sites operating with public subsidies—and the nation would be stuck with its old, inefficient, and highly polluting coal plants. Alternatively, the government could mandate that, after a certain date, *all* coal power plants must capture and store carbon dioxide. Yet what would happen in the overwhelmingly likely event that the specified date arrived and most coal plants simply weren't ready? Would regulators shut down non-compliant plants, reducing the nation's electricity supply by a substantial percentage? Or would the utility operators face stiff fines—which they would quickly pass along to consumers in the form of higher rates? Or would the government simply push the date for compliance back—and back—and back?

Meanwhile, leading climate scientists are warning that we need to reduce CO_2 in the atmosphere below current levels; how high will CO_2 levels rise while we wait for "clean coal" technology to come online?

It might also be argued that partial deployment of carbon capture and storage technology would be better than nothing—at least some carbon emissions would be avoided. However, there is a problem there, too. The research and development costs for limited implementation are likely to be almost as high as for universal deployment (since the technology has to be made to work on a small scale before it can be built out on a large scale). This would represent an enormous investment in an energy source and a technology with a limited future. And that investment will be needed elsewhere.

Coal gasification plants without carbon capture would be less polluting and more efficient than current power plants, but, once again, the up-front costs are very high (and this is why several potential IGCC projects have been canceled or rejected in recent years).

The ongoing, relentless depletion of our nation's—and the world's—coal, oil, and natural gas resources will force us to depend increasingly upon renewable energy. By the end of this century, America will have an essentially all-renewable economy, whether or not we have planned for it. Over the short term, more electricity could come from natural gas, but it is unclear how long the current gas glut will last, given that the new, unconventional sources responsible for it (especially shale gas) are proving expensive to develop and quick to deplete. Building new nuclear plants will be costly and slow—and controversial. And uranium is itself a depleting, non-renewable resource.

But renewable energy sources are not without problems of their own. Their current share of total energy produced is relatively tiny, and a rapid build-up of capacity will require subsidies of some kind. Also, wind and solar power are intermittent, and the times of greatest abundance of sunshine and breeze do not always coincide with times of greatest electricity demand. This is a problem that can probably be solved, but not without an enormous upgrade to the nation's electricity grid. Still other investments in national transport, food-system, and housing infrastructure will be needed to get us to a low-consuming, renewable energy future.

Altogether, it is hard to avoid the conclusion that the years ahead are likely to see increasingly expensive electricity, if not actual shortages. By mid-century, renewables must be ready to provide a substantial majority of energy consumed, or energy shortages could be rampant. An even faster transition will be needed if the nation's goal is (as it should be) to reduce atmospheric carbon dioxide to 350 parts per million, as climate scientist James Hansen says is necessary (currently, we're at 387 ppm, and rising by over 2 ppm per year).

Given a depleting resource base and the likelihood of soaring coal prices, the "clean coal" debate hinges on the question, *Can we afford to do it all?* That is, can we spend tens or hundreds of billions of dollars mitigating the impacts from burning increasingly expensive, depleting coal using expensive coal gasification power plants and unproven carbon capture and storage technologies, while at the same time spending hundreds of billions to develop an entirely different energy infrastructure that we will eventually be forced to rely upon as coal runs out? It would be nice to think so, but the harsh reality is that time and capital are both limited.

Abandoning "clean coal" need not be seen as a retreat in the effort to reduce carbon dioxide emissions. As a nation, we could simply halt the construction of new coal power plants. We could tax carbon. We could cap carbon emissions and ration or sell emissions permits. We could discourage coal mining by enforcing reasonable environmental regulations. None of these strategies would require substantial new investments by the government, just tough policy decisions.

There are other strong arguments against "clean coal." The mining of coal results in environmental, social, and economic ruin for communities in coal regions—witness the travesty of "mountaintop removal" mining practices in Appalachia. Capturing and storing the carbon from coal would do nothing to address that concern. Also, some doubt whether the carbon dioxide that is sequestered underground will really stay there.

While these arguments may be valid, they are unlikely to be decisive in the "clean coal" debate. That debate will be won or lost on the hard, practical basis of cost. And on that basis, the case for "clean coal" may have just fallen apart.

Tough Energy Choices

What would be a sound energy policy from both an energy supply and a climate standpoint? Unfortunately, there are no easy answers. Given the need for rapid reduction in the use of carbon fuels and the expense of building renewable energy infrastructure, energy conservation will almost certainly have to be the basis of our national strategy. This means finding ways to do more with less through increased energy efficiency—but it also means identifying and simply curtailing non-essential current energy consumption. Our climate and energy problems would become much easier to solve if America were to go on an energy diet so that it required only half, a third, or even a quarter of the energy it currently uses. Such demand reductions are certainly possible, but they would require fundamental changes in citizens' habits and expectations, as well as massive investments in efficient technologies—from household gadgets to power plants and transport systems.

Investment will also be required in renewable energy sources, many of which are not currently cost-competitive with fossil fuels. If we wait for market signals to change so that alternative energy is cheaper in every instance (either because fossil fuels have depleted or renewable technology has advanced), we will have waited too long. It will take decades to fully replace the energy systems that power our society. Unless we begin now, the lights may begin to go out in a couple of decades—at about the same time we may be facing climate catastrophe.

All we have to do to realize that horrific future is to continue doing what we are doing now.

"*Unfortunately, coal is . . . one of the most polluting sources of energy available, jeopardizing our health and our environment.*"

Coal Should Not Be the Energy of the Future

Sierra Club

Founded in 1892, the Sierra Club is the nation's oldest environmental organization. In the following viewpoint, the Sierra Club states that coal is a profoundly hazardous source of energy. Coal mining, it argues, rips apart the land, taints water and air, and contributes to global warming. The pollution from coal power plants, the organization maintains, creates smog that harms the human respiratory system and deposits large quantities of lead, arsenic, and mercury into the environment. Moreover, the Sierra Club asserts, coal combustion waste may not be safely contained, and the benefits of clean-coal technologies are unproven.

As you read, consider the following questions:

1. Why is mountaintop removal coal mining destructive, in the words of the Sierra Club?

2. How does particle pollution from coal power plants harm the environment after it settles, as claimed by the author?

3. What are the Sierra Club's arguments against liquid coal?

It was more than 100 years ago on the shores of the lower East River in New York City that [inventor] Thomas Edison opened the Pearl Street Station, the first centralized coal-fired power plant to come on line. More than a century later, coal-fired power plants produce about half of our nation's electricity, and in 2006 a record 1.161 billion tons of coal was mined, most of which went directly to electricity generation. Unfortunately, coal is also one of the most polluting sources of energy available, jeopardizing our health and our environment.

Pollution created by generating electricity from coal does not start or stop at the power plant. It stretches all the way from the coal mine to long after coal is burned and the electricity has been used in our homes and businesses. Mining and burning coal scars lungs, tears up the land, pollutes water, devastates communities, and makes global warming worse.

Mining Hazards

Coal mining causes irreparable harm to our lands, water, and air, and also jeopardizes the health, safety, and economy of nearby communities. In the most destructive type of coal mining, known as mountaintop removal coal mining, a coal company literally blasts apart the tops of mountains to reach thin seams of coal buried below and then, to minimize waste disposal costs, dumps millions of tons of waste rock into the valleys and streams below, causing permanent damage to the ecosystem and landscape. This destructive practice has damaged or destroyed approximately 1,200 miles of streams, disrupted drinking water supplies, flooded communities, damaged homes, eliminated forests, and jeopardizes tourism and recreation.

Coal mining is a major source of water pollution, causing acid mine drainage which occurs when abandoned mines fill with water that mixes with heavy metals and then leaks out into groundwater and streams. Coal preparation, or "washing," also causes water pollution when chemicals and water are used to separate impurities from mined coal. Up to 90 million gallons of coal preparation slurry are produced every year in the U.S., most of which are stored in large waste pits known as impoundments. Impoundments leak into local water supplies and can even burst dramatically, sending millions of gallons of wastes barreling down in mudflows and destroying property and lives.

Additionally, coal mining causes air pollution, including dust and particle pollution that can cause respiratory problems like black lung in coal miners. Coal-laden railcars blow coal dust into the air, causing breathing problems and dirtying the landscape of local communities. Coal mining also causes global warming pollution when it releases heat-trapping methane [gas] found in coal seams.

Burning Coal: US Power Plants

Coal-fired power plants are one of the largest sources of air pollution in the U.S. The consequences for human health are staggering, especially with regards to particle pollution or soot, one of the most deadly types of air pollution in our country. Soot can trigger heart attacks and strokes, worsen asthma, cause irregular heartbeat, and lead to premature death. Many scientific studies have also shown that communities of color are disproportionately exposed to harmful air pollution, including pollution from coal-fired power plants. The damages from particle pollution continue after it has settled to the ground, where it causes acidification of waters, soil nutrient depletion and destruction of forests and crops.

Not only are coal-fired power plants a major source of soot pollution, they are also one of the largest contributors to smog in the nation. In addition to health effects like increased risk of asthma attacks, permanent lung damage, and premature death, smog also harms plants and trees. Persistent smog pollution can alter and disrupt plant growth over time, leading to an estimated $500 million loss due to reduced crop production in the U.S. every year.

Additionally, coal-fired power plants emit large quantities of toxic air pollutants such as lead and arsenic, and are one of the largest sources of man-made mercury pollution in the U.S. Mercury, which enters our food chain after it rains down into our streams and lakes, poisons fish and seafood and accumulates in the animals and people who eat them. Mercury pollution causes brain damage, mental retardation, and other developmental problems in unborn children and infants, and has been linked to a greater risk of coronary heart disease in men. The mercury problem in the U.S. is so widespread that every year one in six women of childbearing age has mercury levels in her blood high enough to put her baby at risk.

Burning coal also releases carbon dioxide (CO_2) pollution, a primary culprit in global warming. Even though coal-fired power plants generate just about half of our nation's electricity, they account for almost 40 percent of our nation's carbon dioxide pollution from all sources, including transportation. In fact, coal-fired power plants have the highest output rate of carbon dioxide (or carbon intensity) per unit of electricity among all fossil fuels.

The Legacy of Coal Combustion

Burning coal for electricity also creates several different types of liquid and solid wastes that are known collectively as coal

combustion wastes. Taken together, the amount of coal combustion wastes produced is staggering: more than 120 million solid tons every year. This waste alone is enough to fill a million railcars every year, or a train that is 9,600 miles long.

Not only is it challenging to find a place to store so much coal combustion waste safely, but even after it is stored coal combustion waste can leak out and pollute the surrounding environment and groundwater. Containing elements like lead, mercury, and arsenic in toxic doses, coal combustion wastes and their pollution have been shown to cause illness and death in plants and animals. In humans, where the greatest exposure risk is from polluted groundwater and drinking water, the toxins have been linked to organ disease, increased cancer, respiratory illness, neurological damage, and developmental problems. In one study, the EPA [Environmental Protection Agency] estimated that more than 21 million people, including more than six million children, lived within five miles of a coal-fired power plant, a daunting figure considering that most coal combustion wastes are stored onsite.

"Clean Coal" Is a Misnomer

The coal industry knows it must change or it will be out of business—that is why it is pushing "clean" coal. But, coal as it exists today is anything but clean.

The supposedly "clean coal" technologies that have attracted the most attention in recent years are carbon capture and sequestration (CCS) and Integrated Gasification Combined Cycle (IGCC). As of now, CCS remains an unproven technology, and experts disagree as to how long it will take for this technology to be available for commercial and wide-scale use. IGCC unfortunately emits just as much global warming pollution as other coal plants.

The coal industry is also pushing liquid coal as a clean alternative, yet liquid coal creates almost double the carbon dioxide emissions per gallon as regular gasoline, and replacing just 10 percent of our nation's fuel with it would require a more than 40 percent increase in coal mining.

The truth is that promises of these and other future technological innovations that will allow us to use coal cleanly are not available today.

The challenge of cleaning up the way we mine and use coal is not small by any means. On average, our country consumes more than three million tons of coal every day, or about 20 pounds of coal for every person in the nation every day of the year. The good news is that we can reduce our dependence on coal by increasing efficiency and relying more on clean energy power like wind and solar, and we can minimize the damage coal causes by ensuring it is mined responsibly, burned cleanly, and does not take us backward on global warming.

> "Coal is a dependable element of energy security, as its use supports the overarching goal of decreasing our dependence on imported energy."

Coal Is the Most Secure Form of Energy

Jude Clemente

Jude Clemente is an energy security analyst and technical writer at San Diego State University's Homeland Security Department. In the following viewpoint, Clemente argues that coal enhances national security in three ways. First, he states that it is a decentralized, easily transportable, and abundant fuel, decreasing the country's dependency on foreign oil. Second, coal power plants provide electricity that is stable in price and availability, he claims, stimulating economic activity and raising the quality of life. Third, Clemente insists that clean-coal technologies dramatically reduce carbon-dioxide emissions and pollutants, minimizing coal's environmental impacts.

Jude Clemente, "The Three National Security Dimensions of Coal," *American Coal*, No. 1, 2010. American Coal Council. Copyright © 2010 American Coal Council. All rights reserved. Reprinted by permission.

As you read, consider the following questions:

1. How does the export potential of clean-coal technologies strengthen US alliances with other nations, in Clemente's opinion?

2. How would a 33 percent decrease in coal-fueled power affect the economy, in the author's view?

3. How do coal power plants today compare with those in 1970s and 1980s, according to Clemente?

The International Energy Agency (IEA) estimates the U.S. has nearly 270 billion tons of recoverable coal reserves, or roughly 250 years remaining at current levels of consumption. These reserves have an energy content exceeding that of the world's known recoverable oil. Coal produces approximately half of the electricity consumed in the U.S. and deposits are found in 38 states. Coal is our single most important domestic energy resource. Coal's contribution to electricity generation is recognized as irreplaceable in the decades ahead. Indeed, a 2008 national public opinion survey sponsored by the American Coalition for Clean Coal Electricity (ACCCE) found:

- 72 percent support the use of coal to generate electricity and 69 percent answered "yes" to the question: "Do you believe coal is a fuel for America's future?"

- 72 percent agree new technologies would allow coal-fueled electricity plants to meet an ultra-low, near zero emissions profile—this includes the widespread deployment of Carbon Capture and Storage (CCS) within the next decade or so

- 84 percent agree the development of new and advanced Clean Coal Technologies (CCTs) offers opportunities to create high-paying domestic jobs and the ability to export these technologies to other countries

Additionally, as the world's fastest growing fossil fuel, coal's affordability, availability, and reliability provide us a unique national security angle to gain allies abroad in "The Global War on Terrorism." The export potential of CCTs, as they continuously develop, is a vital strategy to deepen our defense alliances by preparing others for the inevitable global transition to a low-carbon economy. Every one of the United Nations Millennium Development Goals has access to electricity as a necessary prerequisite. [T]he world is once again turning to coal-fueled generation for incremental supply—reliability and low cost make it integral to global development.

Thus, the support of CCTs is the support of domestic clean energy and a critical national security stance for all Americans. The current Administration strongly supports this position:

"Carbon capture and storage technologies hold enormous potential to reduce our [greenhouse gas] emissions as we power our economy with domestically produced and secure energy," President Barack Obama said.

The present analysis delineates why the continued use of coal through the development of clean coal technologies directly supports the three dimensions of our established national security objective of enhancing: 1) energy security, 2) economic security, and 3) environmental security.

Energy Security

In 2008, the U.S. Department of Energy's (DOE) National Energy Technology Laboratory (NETL) noted the opposition to the construction of new coal-fueled power plants was leading to capacity shortages in many parts of the country and endangering U.S. energy security. "The current opposition to baseload power, and in particular coal-fueled plants, in anticipation of climate change legislation, will have serious and damaging implications for the reliability of electricity supply and the viability of the U.S. economy," NETL reports.

Coal is a dependable element of energy security, as its use supports the overarching goal of decreasing our dependence on imported energy. Shortly after the terrorist attacks of Sept. 11, 2001, the National Academy of Sciences, our most prestigious scientific organization, conducted a detailed analysis of the vulnerabilities of the main U.S. energy sources—nuclear power, oil, natural gas, coal, and the electric power system itself. The Academy indicates coal is clearly the least vulnerable to terrorist attack.

Coal is safely and easily transported and does not require complex pipelines that must be expensively protected (unlike oil and natural gas). Coal's sources and uses are decentralized, thereby presenting a smaller target for enemies. The utilization of coal is an inherent buffer against supply disruptions because it is typically stored at power generating facilities.

The U.S. Department of Defense (DOD) regards coal as a proven source of energy security largely due to its unmatched fuel flexibility. Coal-to-liquids (CTL) technology was used by Germany's armed forces during World War II and commercial production has been ongoing in South Africa since the 1950s. The Office of the Secretary of Defense Initiative and The Defense Energy Support Center illustrate the DOD's commitment to developing alternative liquid fuels derived from secure domestic resources, such as coal.

Currently, the DOD uses nine different petroleum-based fuels for its jet engines, gas turbines, and diesel engine applications and has a goal of developing a single battle space fuel for all branches of the Military. The U.S. Air Force consumes approximately 10 percent of the total jet fuel in the U.S and is acutely aware of the significant advantages of CTL fuels, which can be produced to military specifications. The U.S. Navy is interested in alternative transportation fuels for ships and aircraft. The U.S. Army is testing synthetic fuels in tactical vehicles and generators. The DOD purchases more jet fuel than any other organization in the world and serves as an incentive and catalyst for a commercial CTL industry to produce clean fuels for the Military.

In stark contrast to other proposed solutions, CTL conversion utilizes mature technologies and has known costs. Investments in liquid coal will only become more profitable because rising global demand and declining resources ensure oil prices will continuously increase. Indeed, the IEA supports CTL plants because they can "bear the higher cost of CCS and establish a CO_2 transport and storage infrastructure that can subsequently be applied to power generation facilities." RAND Corporation concludes CTL utilization is "feasible at crude oil prices well below the prices seen in 2007 and 2008." [T]he 3 million barrels per day CTL industry proposed by RAND could help supplant risky or now fading sources of U.S. crude oil imports.

Economic Security

Generating a half of all U.S. electricity, coal is one of our least expensive energy resources. We have consistently relied upon coal to meet growing demand and moderate energy costs for families and businesses. Coal provides stability in both price and availability. Coal sustains our economy because it is readily affordable, available, and reliable. In fact, coal-fueled electricity has been the cornerstone of the economic empowerment and rising quality of life generations of Americans have enjoyed since the turn of the last century.

Research by Schurr and Jorgenson (1994) indicated that falling electricity prices (largely credited to the use of coal) were at least as important to the productivity growth of the U.S. economy during the 1980s and 1990s as the development of computer technologies. Research by the Center for Energy and Economic Development and others have shown the substantial benefits delivered by coal-fueled power plants and the economic damage that would result if new laws force a reduction in use.

For example, a 2006 study by Penn State University analyzed the economic benefits of coal and the potential impact of replacing coal with less reliable, more costly energy sources, such as natural gas and a 10 percent renewable energy mix. Research suggests that by 2015:

- The benefit of coal use per year at current project levels is expected to be more than $1 trillion in gross domestic product (GDP)—$360 billion in additional household income and nearly 7 million jobs

- A 33 percent decrease in coal-fueled power generation would lower our GDP by $166 billion, household income by $64 billion, and the employment level by 1.2 million people than what would exist otherwise

- A 66 percent decrease in coal-fueled power generation would reduce GDP by $371 billion, household income by $142 billion, and employment by 2.7 million people

Coal is giving more and more people across the globe an opportunity to step into the modern world. Developing countries, most notably China and India, are specifically committing to coal. Its reliability and low cost have rescued literally hundreds of millions of people from the depths of abject poverty. Further, these two nations, holding nearly 40 percent of humanity, will require unprecedented levels of energy to sustain their growing economies. Their extensive supplies of coal can help us stave off the geopolitical tension increased competition for resources will surely ignite. Both China and India have relatively small oil and natural gas reserves.

The security, stability, and availability of coal help mitigate price shocks in global energy markets. A national CTL program, for instance, would decrease our exposure to the world's precarious oil market and lessen the impact of a supply disruption. Additionally, every produced barrel of unconventional liquid fuel lowers the price of oil and reduces revenues for major global suppliers—several of which use "petrodollars" to fund terrorism and/or spread anti-democratic ideals.

The coal industry is a leading sector in many states and has a long history of high-paying job creation. America's massive coal endowment is a strategic resource whose economic value in the digital age will be as great as it was in the industrial age. Technologies to use coal cleanly and capture carbon dioxide will be in high demand around the world—creating millions of jobs and other economic opportunities. The U.S. Department of Commerce conservatively projects global demand for CCTs will reach $260 billion from 2003–2030 alone.

Environmental Security

Even the opponents of coal recognize the inherent value of the fuel and the importance of CCTs. Former U.S. Vice President Al Gore has stated: "When the cost of not using it [coal] is calculated, it becomes obvious that CCS will play a significant and growing role as one of the major building blocks of a solution to the climate crisis." CCS technology, once fully demonstrated at utility scale, will be broadly deployed rather quickly. Government support of these imperative projects is materializing:

> The Obama administration's economic stimulus package, The American Recovery and Reinvestment Act of 2009, sets aside $2.4 billion to expand and accelerate the commercial deployment of CCS. The American Clean Energy and Security Act of 2009, which passed through the U.S. House of Representatives and is now being debated in the U.S. Senate, also offers key provisions that will facilitate the demonstration and deployment of CCS power plants.

> "Prosperity depends upon reliable, affordable access to energy. Coal . . . is likely to be a major and growing source of electricity generation for the foreseeable future. . . . We must make it our goal to advance carbon capture and storage

technology to the point where widespread, affordable deployment can begin in 8 to 10 years," said Steve Chu, Secretary of Energy.

The European Union recognizes commercial CCS as enough of an emerging reality it wants all coal-fueled power plants to be fitted with CCS technology by 2020. The G-8 nations strongly support launching 20 large-scale CCS demonstration projects around the globe, with the goal of beginning broad deployment by 2020. Just as importantly, the IEA supports the 2020 target date.

Rajendra Pachauri, chair of the Intergovernmental Panel on Climate Change (IPCC), the voice of authority on climate change, also encourages an expanded role for CCTs: "They [CCS projects] will work, I see no reason why a technology of that nature will be anywhere beyond human capabilities." With coal's dominant position in poverty reduction assured in the decades ahead, he believes all that is lacking for widespread CCS is the political will to commit to commercial deployment by 2020. The benefits involved are profound; Pachauri's native country, India, has some 400 million people without access to electricity (the IEA reports the figure worldwide is 1.5 billion).

From gasification to sulfur-capturing scrubbers, the effect the wide range of CCTs is having on electricity generation is comparable to the influence microprocessors had on computers. "CCTs have been developed and deployed to reduce the environmental impact of coal utilization over the past 30 to 40 years," says the IEA, the operator of a Clean Coal Center. The U.S. coal industry has a proven track record of developing technological pathways to successfully address environmental concerns.

Power plants built today emit 90 percent fewer criteria emissions than those they displace from the 1970s. Since 1980, CCTs have slashed power plant emissions by 54 percent, despite a 71 percent increase in coal-fueled generation. With even steeper reductions on the horizon, the total opposition to coal projects across-the-board greatly impedes the deployment of more advanced plants capable of reining in nearly all emissions. The IPCC confirms current CCT technologies can already capture approximately 85–95 percent of the carbon dioxide (CO_2) processed in a capture plant. The result is a power plant with CCS could reduce CO_2 emissions by 80–90 percent compared to a plant without CCS.

In 2008, the DOE reported the U.S. has the capacity to store 3,900 billion tons of CO_2 at 230 different underground sites. Considering the U.S. emits 6–7 billion tons of CO_2 every year, this means ample space exists to store 100 percent of its emissions for approximately 560 years. According to the IPCC, properly managed geological formations are likely to retain more than 99 percent of the injected CO_2 for over 1,000 years. CO_2 becomes much less mobile over time. Indeed, CCS is a prime example of the unique opportunity we have to simultaneously enhance U.S. energy security and mitigate the adverse effects of climate change.

Conclusion

Due to record oil prices, the constraints on nuclear energy, the volatility of natural gas prices, and the inherent limitations of renewable energy, coal is the standout choice to: 1) meet the inevitable rise in electricity demand and 2) enhance energy security. CCTs extend our energy self-reliance and will solidify coal's critical position in the U.S. energy system in the switchover to a low-carbon economy. As the U.S. Air Force puts it, we can "neutralize a national security threat by tapping into the country's abundant coal reserves."

"The nuclear industry has the most culture of safety around it of any industry."

Nuclear Power Is the Most Secure Form of Energy

Patrick Moore, as told to Michael Kanellos

Patrick Moore is chair of the Clean and Safe Energy Coalition, and he was a founding member of Greenpeace. Michael Kanellos is editor in chief at Greentech Media and a former staff writer at CNET. In the following viewpoint, Moore discusses with Kanellos how nuclear energy is more secure and safe than coal. Nuclear power plants are closely monitored and built to withstand catastrophic assaults, Moore maintains. In addition, he suggests that international partnerships will prevent countries from using enrichment technologies for nuclear weapons. And compared with coal facilities, Moore points out, nuclear power plants produce no regulated air emissions, release less radiation, and have an outstanding track record of safety.

As you read, consider the following questions:

1. Why did Moore initially oppose nuclear energy?

2. How does Moore respond to the nuclear accident at Three Mile Island?

3. What is the outlook on fuel for nuclear energy, as stated by Moore?

Patrick Moore seems to court controversy.

Decades ago, he helped found Greenpeace, which fought nuclear proliferation and promoted environmental causes. But for the last several years, he has been an outspoken advocate of nuclear power as well as a critic of the environmental movement.

He now co-chairs the Clean and Safe Energy Coalition, a nuclear industry group, with former New Jersey Governor Christine Whitman.

Although nuclear power remains highly controversial, it's also making a comeback as concerns about global warming and electricity prices rise. Sixteen organizations are expected to file applications to build 31 new reactors in the U.S. Nuclear was a big topic at the World Economic Forum at Davos [Switzerland].

Moore spoke with CNET News.com's Michael Kanellos about the potential for nuclear power as well as where he thinks environmentalists went wrong.

An Important Distinction

Michael Kanellos: When people look at your biography and see you're a Greenpeace co-founder and now a nuclear advocate, they don't believe it. Could you give us a synopsis of your personal history on this issue?

Patrick Moore: Well, actually I did feel a little lonely in that corner for a while, but I've been joined by the likes of Stewart Brand, Jared Diamond (author of *Guns, Germs, and Steel*), and (environmental author) Tim Flannery, and now we form a fairly serious phalanx of pro-nuclear environmentalists. In fact, I'm the honorary chair of the Canadian chapter of Environmentalists for Nuclear Energy, which has 9,000 members worldwide.

As a co-founder of Greenpeace, even though I was a scientist, I made the same mistake in those days as all the rest of my colleagues did. We kind of lumped nuclear energy in with nuclear weapons as if all things nuclear were evil. It was an honest mistake. We were totally focused on the threat of nuclear war during the Cold War. Nuclear testing was what Greenpeace started on and we were peaceniks, and I think it's fair to say that the antinuclear-energy movement to some extent was formed out of the peace movement.

But in retrospect, I believe we failed to make an important distinction between the peaceful versus the destructive uses of a technology. There are many technologies that are very good that can be used for destructive purposes. Cars can be made into car bombs as long as you have a little bit of fertilizer and diesel oil. Machetes have killed more people than any other weapon in the last 20 years, over a million, and yet they're the most important tool for farmers in the developing world.

It wasn't until after I'd left Greenpeace and the climate change issue started coming to the forefront that I started rethinking energy policy in general and realized that I had been incorrect in my analysis of nuclear as being some kind of evil plot. The perception at the time that nuclear energy equaled nuclear weapons was to some extent based on the fact that the only exception to the separation of peaceful and military nuclear technology was when India bought a reactor from Canada and then broke their promise and used that peaceful reactor to make plutonium to make their first weapon.

Terrorism and Safety

Make the case for nuclear power. It emits far less greenhouse gases than coal, but there are the disposal issues.

Well, it's not only cleaner, it's almost infinitely cleaner in that it has no regulated air emissions. Coal actually releases far more radiation than nuclear plants. There is some radiation released by the nuclear industry, but it's not considered to be of any significance from a health point of view or an environmental point of view. It is cost-effective and it is proven safe. Safety and waste are the two main concerns.

Greenpeace keeps harping on the terrorist issue, but the fact is the nuclear plants in the United States were designed from the beginning to withstand a 747 [airliner crashing into them]. They are the hardest targets in the United States from a security point of view. They are very closely watched and monitored and they are built in such a way that they are not really a very desirable target. The World Trade Center was a much more desirable target and so were many other political targets and many other industrial targets. So that isn't an issue.

But the safety issue?

If people look at the actual record, as opposed to the sensationalist speculation, there has never been a member of the public injured by a nuclear plant in the United States, even during Three Mile Island [a serious nuclear power plant accident in Pennsylvania in 1979]. It was just a bad mechanical failure. It did not cause harm to the public or to the workers in the plant. There is no evidence that anyone was injured by that accident. That was the worst accident in the history of the West, excluding the Soviet Union's stupid Chernobyl design, which is pretty much phased out now, although there are still 11 of them running. [The Chernobyl nuclear power plant accident occurred in April 1986.]

There are that many Chernobyl-style plants left?

Yes, there are 10 in Russia and 1 in Lithuania, but they are all scheduled to be phased out. After Chernobyl, they were all upgraded from a safety point of view. The accident at Chernobyl was a combination of ridiculous operator error. Secondly, they built reactors without containment vessels. No one else has done that. What the Soviets did was they took their military plutonium weapons production reactors and cookie-cuttered them all over the countryside. It was an economic shortcut and they learned the hard way, but the safety record in the West is impeccable in terms of not causing any harm to people.

Six thousand people die in coal mines every year in this world. Look how many people die in car accidents and many of those are innocent passengers and pedestrians. The impact of fossil fuel combustion on public health is the single largest impact of any technology we have.

But if we see more plants being built in the West, doesn't that increase the chance for negligence and people cutting corners? I mean, the more people you have, the more chances for people to mess up you have.

I don't know about that. You cannot build a nuclear plant in this world today without it being world-class in both its design and its operation. It's just not possible to do that. There is too much oversight. There is the International Atomic Energy Agency. There is the fact that these designs are coming out of the United States, France, and Russia. India, too; most people don't realize that India is at the very forefront of nuclear technology, in recycling, in producing thorium fuel, in fast reactors. Their science is as good as anybody else's in the world, and the Chinese are fast becoming a major center for nuclear technology as well. I don't think that that is a risk.

The nuclear industry has the most culture of safety around it of any industry. In the States it's safer to work in a nuclear plant than it is to work in either real estate or financial services, according to the Bureau of Labor Statistics. . . .

A Place on the Grid

A lot of people will agree with the state of nuclear technology but will argue that we should put more money into solar ther-

mal or solar photovoltaic first and see if we can make progress there before we go to nuclear. What do you say to that?

Well, I don't see how they are mutually exclusive. We know how to build nuclear plants. We don't know how to build solar thermal plants that operate cost effectively and we don't even know if we can build a solar thermal plant that will go through 5 or 10 days of cloud cover. I am all in favor of investing in solar thermal, but I think it has to be on a measured R&D [research and development] basis, and I would like to see it coming under 10 cents a kilowatt-hour.

Solar photovoltaic simply has no place on the grid. All the money that's going into subsiding solar is a waste of money because it could be being used on more effective technologies that we already have that are not unreliable and intermittent. The $3.2 billion that California is subsidizing in solar would build a 1,000-MW nuclear plant and provide 10 times as much power into the system and on a reliable basis.

Many claim that nuclear is actually the only source of power that is going up in price. These aren't environmental advocates. These are Wall Street analysts. The nuclear energy industry says the opposite. Who is right here?

Well, the price of the plants is going up in terms of the capital costs, but then everything is going up. Concrete is going up; steel is going up. It's true that nuclear has a higher capital cost than the fossil energy plants, but it has a lower operating cost once it is established.

A compact fluorescent light bulb costs five times as much as an incandescent light bulb, but it only costs a fifth as much to run it and it lasts a lot longer. So it is a good investment. The trouble with individuals is that they want to (be paid) back in 2 years. Big institutions don't mind an 8- or 10-year payback and nuclear provides that.

Is the public perception changing? Do you find more people saying they will consider nuclear or people who are actually in favor of it?

A considerable majority of Americans are in favor of nuclear energy. It's around 70 percent of the general public. (Editor's note: An MIT [Massachusetts Institute of Technology] survey last year [2007] said only 35 percent of Americans wanted to see nuclear power increase.) The closer you get to an operating nuclear plant, the higher the support is. The average within 10 miles of a plant is 80 percent in the U.S. In some plants, it's up to 90 percent because the people living near them know that they have operated safely and that they're a huge wealth generator in the community. They are basically a very compact wealth generating machine, producing energy and producing employment in communities. They say the closer you go to a nuclear reactor, the better the schools and the roads are.

How about "Not in my backyard"-ism? Although people support nuclear, they also say they want to see the plants 500 miles away.

The good news there is that the first (likely) wave of new plants will all be built on existing sites. There is, in fact, a huge amount of room to expand on the existing sites. Many of these sites were originally designed for eight reactors and only have two on them.

Some people have suggested exploiting the waste heat in these factories to make hydrogen or purify water.

There are additional benefits beyond just giving electricity. And we will use the electricity to charge all our plug-in hybrids. We are going to need more electricity in the future for that. It doesn't make sense to charge a battery with a coal-fired power plant from an air pollution or climate point of view.

There's no possibility that California can meet its objectives without new nuclear, either in or out of state to supply the electricity. Twenty percent of the state's electricity now comes from coal-fired power plants. If you cut that 20 percent out, you simply cannot replace that with renewables unless they can make solar thermal work. They should go ahead, try it, but in the meantime build some nuclear plants. That is the only way that a full umbilical cord can be cut.

What do you think of wave power?

It is so pie-in-the-sky that we shouldn't even think about it. Just let people test it. If they can figure out how to make it work, fine. But I don't really see that much promise in all those tidal- and wave-powered programs. . . .

Disposal, Supply, and Enrichment

How about the nuclear waste disposal? Has there been much progress technologically?

It is not a problem technologically. It's called recycling, or what used to be called reprocessing. The French, the Russians, the Japanese all use it. It is basically separating out the remaining uranium and the plutonium that is manufactured as a byproduct and used as fuel again.

Plutonium is a fuel; we don't need to wait 250,000 years for it to decay. We can use it right away as a fuel and turn it into fission products, which will then only have a 300-year lifespan of being radioactive. Japan just opened a $30 billion fuel fabrication and recycling center in Northern Honshu. Japan figured out a way to take the French technology, which is probably the leading technology, and design a system in which the plutonium never emerges as a pure product anywhere; it's only inside, where nobody could, without dying, get it. The plutonium is separated, then before it comes out it's recombined with uranium into what's called mixed-oxide fuel, which cannot be made into a bomb.

How does the supply of fuel look?

Fifty percent of all the nuclear energy being produced in the United States is from dismantled Soviet warheads. We are turning swords to plowshares, not the other way around. There is enough enriched uranium and plutonium in (missile) stockpiles that is surplus now to (fill) the needs of the military to run our nuclear plants for years. When you start recycling, it magnifies the fuel reserve by 5 to 10 times. So we've actually got a thousand years of nuclear fuel for the existing reactors. The mining industry actually stopped looking for uranium 30 years ago because there already was enough discovered.

Now, they're looking for it again and finding it all over the place in places they didn't know it existed. There's a huge find in Labrador, Canada, for example. Slovakia has now been proven to have the largest uranium reserve in all of Western Europe. Austria still has tons of the stuff, and now Kazakhstan has come on as a major world's supplier.

Before we run out of uranium, there's a lot of people interested in the thorium fuel cycle. Thorium is much more abundant in the earth than uranium, so it's another nuclear fuel that is proven to be workable. India is well advanced in this technology and there is an international group of thorium scientists that is meeting on a regular basis.

One last thing. How about the rogue state question? People worry about states like Iran getting bomb-making capabilities. Is the regulatory framework strong enough to take care of that?

There is a group of academics from the U.S. and Europe who have come up with the proposal to create a kind of insurance policy for the nuclear fuel supply. The idea is to restrict the amount of enrichment technology because you can use uranium enrichment technology centrifuges to either make nuclear fuel or a nuclear bomb. So there is a big interest in reducing the number of facilities that do enrichment and basically in keeping them in the existing weapon states, which is where they are now except for Iran.

There is also the Global Nuclear Energy Partnership otherwise known as GNEP, which 20-odd countries are part of. It wants control over the front end, which is uranium enrichment, and the back end, or recycling plutonium, to maintain control over those processes in such a way that countries that don't have those technologies are guaranteed a supply of fuel.

It's really interesting, in some ways, how this whole nuclear renaissance is causing a new alignment of interests around the world.

Periodical Bibliography

The following articles have been selected to supplement the diverse views presented in this chapter.

Jeffrey Ball	"Coal Hard Facts: Cleaning It Won't Be Dirt Cheap," *Wall Street Journal*, March 20, 2009.
Ari Berman	"The Dirt on Clean Coal," *Nation*, March 26, 2009.
Richard Conniff	"The Myth of Clean Coal," *Yale Environment 360*, June 3, 2008.
Kent Garber	"Why Clean Coal Is Years Away," *U.S. News & World Report*, March 17, 2009.
Veronique Greenwood	"The Lesser Evil: Nuclear or Coal?," *Seed Magazine*, July 2, 2009.
Mason Inman	"Mining the Truth on Coal Supplies," *National Geographic News*, September 8, 2010.
Christine MacDonald	"Is This the End for Coal?," *E: The Environmental Magazine*, September/October 2009.
Christy van der Merwe	"Coal on Its Way to a Cleaner Future," *Mining Weekly*, August 28, 2009.
Syd S. Peng	"Understanding the Chinese Coal Industry," *Coal Age*, August 26, 2010.
James Ridgeway	"Scrubbing King Coal," *Mother Jones*, May/June 2008.
Rebecca Terrell	"Clean Energy: The Nuclear Solution," *New American*, June 8, 2010.
Jeff Wallace	"Coal Is Here for the Long Haul," *American Coal*, Issue 1, 2010.

OPPOSING
VIEWPOINTS®
SERIES

CHAPTER 2

Is Coal Use Justified?

Chapter Preface

Coal that is liquefied and processed into gasoline, diesel, or aviation fuel is known as coal-to-liquid (CTL) fuel or liquid coal. It is created in two ways: direct liquefaction and indirect liquefaction. In the former, coal is dissolved at high temperature and pressure in a solvent and refined later. In indirect liquefaction, the coal is gasified into a synthetic gas—a combination of hydrogen and carbon dioxide—and then condensed using the Fischer-Tropsch process, which was developed by German chemists Franz Fischer and Hans Tropsch in the 1920s.

Though it was commercialized in Germany in 1936, CTL fuels have not been used widely. In World War II, Germany relied on liquid coal after Allied forces cut off its oil supplies. In the 1950s, South Africa turned to the Fischer-Tropsch process and domestic coal for fuel when it faced anti-apartheid sanctions on oil imports. And in the 1970s, former president Jimmy Carter supported CTL fuels amid America's petroleum crisis, resulting in demonstration projects to show the process's feasibility. Today, only South Africa has a commercial liquid-coal industry; an estimated 30 percent of its gasoline and diesel supplies are derived from coal, according to the World Coal Association.

The production of liquid coal is expensive, but the instability of the oil market in recent years has regenerated interest in the fuel, which can power existing automobiles, public transportation, and commercial airliners. In fact, according to a December 4, 2006, *Newsweek* article, worldwide production of liquid coal is projected to jump from 150,000 barrels a day today to 600,000 barrels a day in 2020 and 1.8 million barrels a day in 2030. As of October 2010, developers are seeking $2 billion in public-loan guarantees from the US Department of Energy to build the nation's first CTL plant in Wyoming, which was proposed in 2006.

Nonetheless, liquid coal is controversial. Opponents claim that it will bring environmental and social disaster, while supporters insist that it is an alternative to oil that is ecological and abundant. In the following chapter, the authors argue the advantages and disadvantages of having the synthetic fuel and coal as integral parts of the nation's energy profile.

> *"Coal is a major source of air pollution, mining accidents, and environmental damage. Unfortunately, we can't live without it."*

Coal Is a Necessity

Michael Kanellos

Michael Kanellos is editor in chief at Greentech Media and a former staff writer at CNET. In the following viewpoint, Kanellos maintains that coal is a necessary part of the world's energy profile. It currently accounts for half of the electricity generated in the United States, he asserts, and adds that the demand for coal—among emerging economies such as India and China—will increase 28 percent by 2030. Therefore, Kanellos insists, researching and developing technologies to clean up coal—from removing pollutants to carbon capture and sequestration—may be the only practical solution to adapt to climate change.

As you read, consider the following questions:

1. What are the 2006 estimates of the world's coal supplies, as stated by Kanellos?

2. How does coal affect pollution, according to Kanellos?

3. What does the SkyMine process achieve, as described by the author?

Coal is a major source of air pollution, mining accidents, and environmental damage. Unfortunately, we can't live without it.

The coal question remains perhaps the largest and most difficult issue in the clean-tech and energy world. Proponents of solar, wind, and even nuclear power tout themselves as cleaner and safer alternatives. Environmental activists and many scientists also warn that "clean coal" technologies will only dupe the public into a false sense of security.

On the other hand, coal use continues to climb, particularly in China. Clean coal technologies, along with carbon capture and sequestration, may be the only practical way to adapt to climate change. The profits, moreover, are potentially massive.

"Clean coal is the biggest opportunity" in clean tech, said Stephan Dolezalek, a partner at VantagePoint Venture Partners earlier this year [2007]. "If you can solve that problem, it will be bigger than Google."

The Basics of Coal

What are those opportunities? They are mostly on the drawing board now. Here's a primer on the basics of coal:

How much coal is there? Approximately 998 billion tons of recoverable coal sits underground, according to a 2006 estimate from the International Energy Agency. The U.S. has the most, with 268 billion tons, followed by Russia (173 billion tons), China (126 billion tons) and India (102 billion tons). The four collectively hold 67 percent of the recoverable reserves.

In 2006, 1,438 U.S. mines produced 1.163 billion short tons of coal, according to the U.S. Department of Energy, a 2.8 percent increase from the year before. A short ton is 2,000 pounds.

A ton of coal, depending on the grade, has as much heat energy (25 million BTUs [British thermal units]) as 4.5 barrels of oil. There are probably only 1.9 trillion barrels of conventional oil left for human consumption, and not all of it can be recovered. Thus, there's more than twice as much coal out there [as] oil.

How fast is demand growing? Steadily, but ominously. Coal accounted for 26 percent of energy consumed in 2004 worldwide, according to the U.S. Energy Information Agency [EIA], and will grow to 28 percent by 2030. Total energy consumption, however, will be going up a few percentage points a year, so in that same period of time, coal consumption will rise a whopping 74 percent, from 114.4 quadrillion BTUs to 199 quadrillion BTUs.

India and China will account for 72 percent of the increase, but coal consumption is expected to also rise in Russia, South Africa, and the U.S. The U.S. is something of a wild card. With carbon taxes and more alternative energy, the growth could decline, but coal will still be a big part of the energy profile.

"Ninety percent of the fossil fuel reserves in the U.S., India, and China are in coal, and China and India are not going to move from this fuel in the future," said Jeremy Carl, a research fellow in the program for Energy and Sustainable Development at Stanford University. "They are not going to turn off the lights."

China last year [in 2006] erected 90 gigawatts' worth of coal plants last year alone, Carl noted. That's bigger than the electrical grid of the U.K. [United Kingdom]

Where does it get used? Primarily in electrical power plants. In the United States, roughly 1.03 billion tons of the 1.1 billion tons of coal consumed in 2006 got gobbled up by power plants. Coal accounted for 49 percent of the electricity generated in the U.S. in 2006, a slight decline from 2005 due in part to warmer temperatures. (Nuclear power was second, with about 20.2 percent, while natural gas clocked in at 18.8 percent. Solar and wind barely account for 2.4 percent.)

How does coal affect pollution? Coal accounted for 39 percent of carbon dioxide emissions in 2004 (behind oil) but is expected to pass oil for the No. 1 spot in 2010, according to the EIA. Even if the United States were to replace every incandescent bulb in the country with compact fluorescents, the benefits would be eradicated by the carbon dioxide from two coal-fired plants over a year, said Ed Mazria, founder of Architecture 2030. The nonprofit encourages builders, suppliers, and architects to move toward making carbon neutral buildings by 2030.

"The only fossil fuel that can fuel global warming is coal. If you stop coal, you stop global warming. End of story," Mazria said.

Other pollutants include nitrogen compounds, sulfur, aluminum, silicon, and even trace amounts of radioactive materials like uranium. China has banned the use of coal burners in homes in cities like Beijing, but coal pollution remains a large health hazard in the country.

Environmental and health problems include acid rain, polluted water systems, stripped forests, and mining hazards. Deaths attributed to coal range from several hundred to several thousand a year, depending on who does the counting and which respiratory deaths get attributed to coal.

How much does it cost? In the early '70s, natural gas was a cheaper source for generating electricity, but coal surpassed it in 1976 and has been at the bottom ever since. In 2005, generating a million BTUs from coal cost $1.54, compared with $8.20 for natural gas. Coal prices are rising, but so is the cost of everything else. Solar thermal plants, which generate electricity with heat from the sun, are approaching the cost of natural gas plants.

US Clean Coal Leadership

If the technology exists for us to use coal in a clean fashion, then that is something all of us should welcome, particularly because China and India are building coal-fired power plants at a rapid rate, and they likely have lifespans of several decades. Coal is a cheaper resource, and they're going to be figuring out a way to exploit it, so we should help to find technologies that will ensure that if it is used, it is used cleanly. The U.S. is recognized as the global leader in understanding better geologic coal-sequestration technologies. If we abandon that leadership, we risk leaving the rest of the planet wide open to investing billions in polluting infrastructure.

Amanda Little, Grist, *July 30, 2007.*

Cleaning Up Coal

What are some ideas for cleaning up coal?

• Squeeze out the water: CoalTek, which has received funds from Draper Fisher Jurvetson among others, has come up with a way to remove water, sulfur, chlorine, ash, and mercury out of low-grade coal prior to burning it in coal-fired plants. The process thus removes some pollutants and also makes coal more energy intensive, which leads to less coal burned, in turn leading to lower pollutants, said CEO [chief executive officer] Chris Poirier. It has a 120,000-ton-a-year facility in Kentucky and has plans to expand.

Stanford's Carl points to another potential benefit of CoalTek's process. It makes coal more uniform, which makes it easier to burn in a wider variety of plants. In turn, this can cut down on the transportation required to get coal to plants that can burn it, an indirect carbon dioxide benefit.

"There are a hundred different types of things that are called coal, and they all can't be burned in the same place," Carl said.

• Convert it to natural gas: GreatPoint Energy and EnergyQuest, among others, says it can make coal into natural gas, a cleaner fossil fuel, that sells for around $4 per million BTUs, less than the $7 per million BTUs of today. Carbon dioxide produced during the conversion will get sequestered at plants.

Conversion technologies tend to "leak" energy—not all of the potential energy that's originally in coal gets turned into electricity, but some analysts who have studied the process say it has promise, particularly as natural gas prices rise.

The company has built a small demo plant in Iowa and has raised more than $100 million to build larger factories. The first will go up in Somerset, Mass.

The federal government, meanwhile, will put $1.5 billion into the FutureGen project, which hopes to build a pollution-free coal plant that will produce power via gasification and hydrogen, and sequester the carbon dioxide on site. The prototype won't be ready, however, for at least another six years.

• Better boilers: You don't hear much about Fuel-Tech, but it's come up with an interesting niche (reflected in a fourfold rise in the stock price since 2005). It specializes in boilers, chemicals, and other industrial products that cut down on the amount of nitrogen dioxide, sulfur trioxide, carbon dioxide, and other pollutants that get produced in coal burning. The NOxOut process can cut nitrogen oxides by 25 percent to 50 percent; more than 450 companies have installed it.

• Coal to liquids: It could be called the ol' Hans and Franz process. Franz Fischer and Hans Tropsch in the 1920s coined a way to turn coal into a liquid. First the coal is converted to a synthetic gas (basically, the gasification equation for making natural gas) and then converted to a liquid. The high cost of the [Fischer-Tropsch] process, however, has typically made it interesting to people who couldn't get petroleum. The Third

Reich [Nazi Germany] used it in World War II to fuel their tanks, and South Africa cranked up production to avoid apartheid trade barriers.

New catalysts and gasifiers, along with rising gas prices, however, are eroding the price premium. Coal companies have said they can make liquid fuel for around $50 a barrel or less. At the same time, U.S. Sens. Jim Bunning (R-Ky.) and Barack Obama (D-Ill.) are pushing for tax credits. (Syntroleum is trying to use Fischer-Tropsch for animal fat and renewable feedstocks.)

Producing and burning this fuel, however, would result in a massive dose of greenhouse gases. In fact, when the whole process is taken into consideration, liquid fuels derived from coal generate more carbon dioxide than just burning coal itself. If a quarter of the world's coal reserves became liquids, it would increase atmospheric greenhouse gases by 300 parts per million, said Alex Farrell, assistant professor in the energy and resources group at U.C. [University of California] Berkeley. That would more than double the pre-industrial atmospheric concentrations of greenhouse gases. Even with sequestration, gases would rise by 150 parts per million.

Increasing the amount of oil coming from tar sands—which accounts for 3 million barrels of the 80 million barrels consumed a day—would have a similar effect, he added.

"If we do this, I think we are going to have massive increases in the amount of carbons in the atmosphere," he said. If the costs of sequestration and carbon taxes were added, the economic argument also gets substantially weaker.

• The car coal latte: Silverado GreenFuel takes low-grade coal, pulverizes it and cooks it under pressure with water until it develops a waxy coating. The waxy coal particles are then reunited with carbon-infused water removed at an earlier part of the process to make a liquid fuel. The end result is a liquid fuel that would sell for $15 a barrel, if it were oil, the company claims.

Silverado has signed a memorandum of understanding with the state of Mississippi to build a $26 million demonstration plant capable of producing the equivalent of about 111,000 barrels of its "Green Fuel" a year. (Roughly 2.5 barrels of Green Fuel equal a barrel of oil.) The plant is due to open in three years.

"Coal is 200 years of dirty. The proof will be in the pudding," said CEO Gary Anselmo. But it's also unproven on a big scale.

Researchers at Louisiana State University, meanwhile, are trying to develop catalysts and processes that would allow energy companies to convert coal into a mix of carbon monoxide and hydrogen, and then convert those gases into ethanol.

Carbon Capture and Sequestration

What about carbon capture? Since coal can't disappear overnight, several start-ups and industrial giants have gravitated toward ideas for storing carbon dioxide and other pollutants that come from it. Powerspan is building a facility in Sugarland, Texas, that will capture the emissions equal to a 125-megawatt generator. The company has developed a process called Electro-Catalytic Oxidation that filters out nitric oxide, sulfur dioxide, mercury, and fine particles from smokestacks. The remaining carbon dioxide is captured by an ammonia-based solution, which is later recovered.

Then there is Skyonic, which has come up with an industrial process called SkyMine that captures 90 percent of the carbon dioxide coming out of smoke stacks and mixes it with sodium hydroxide to make sodium bicarbonate, or baking soda. The baking soda can then be used as a safe material for landfills or sold to industrial buyers.

"It is cleaner than food-grade (baking soda)," said Joe David Jones, Skyonic's CEO.

The big issue for these companies will be cost—capture systems like this will likely cost tens to hundreds of millions—and how difficult it will be to retrofit existing facilities to accommodate this stuff.

How good is carbon capture and sequestration? No one knows. Ideas range from putting gases into empty, underground chambers and ringing it with warning sensors (plans are being sketched out for trials in North Africa) to pumping it into porous rock formations (where it will bind with rock) or saline aquifers.

The goal of the Southeast Regional Carbon Sequestration Partnership (SECARB), funded by the National Energy Technology Laboratory of the Department of Energy, is to study carbon-dioxide injection and storage capacity of the Tuscaloosa-Woodbine geologic system that stretches from Texas to Florida. The region has the potential to store more than 200 billion tons of the gas, which the department says is equal to about 33 years of emissions.

Beginning in the fall [of 2008], SECARB scientists will start to inject a million tons of carbon dioxide a year into a brine reservoir near Natchez, Miss. The large scale of the project raises questions, though. What about soil contamination, leakage, or earthquakes?

Meanwhile, the clock is ticking.

"We haven't invested in deep research or spent much money in testing out the scenarios. There are a lot of uncertainties," said Jiang Lin, a scientist with the China Sustainable Energy Program with Lawrence Berkeley Lab in a recent speech.

"Without carbon capture and sequestration, we are all toast," Lin added.

"There's no doubt that we're going to see solar as cheap as coal power a lot sooner than many people realize."

The Cost of Solar Energy Will Soon Compare with the Cost of Coal

Mark Clayton

Mark Clayton is a staff writer for the Christian Science Monitor. *In the following viewpoint, Clayton forecasts that solar energy will become cost competitive with coal in the next several years. He claims that researchers are developing solar cells that will boost efficiency and cut power production costs, placing solar in reach of grid parity with coal. With these scientific breakthroughs, more homeowners will install solar panels on their rooftops to take advantage of cheaper electricity and state incentives, the author maintains.*

As you read, consider the following questions:

1. How low must solar power prices fall for it to be competitive with fossil fuels, in Clayton's view?

2. Why is boosting a solar cell's efficiency from 15 to 18 percent significant, in the author's view?

3. What outcomes does Clayton say analysts expect after a "shakeout" in the solar-panel industry?

"Solar power is the energy of the future—and always will be."

That tired joke, which has dogged solar-generated electricity for decades due to its high cost, could be retired far sooner than many think.

While solar contributes less than 1 percent of the energy generated in the United States today, its costs are turning sharply downward.

Whether using mirrors that focus desert sunlight to harvest heat and spin turbines or rooftop photovoltaic panels that turn sunshine directly into current, solar is on track to deliver electricity to residential users at a cost on par with natural gas and perhaps even coal within the next four to seven years, industry experts say.

"We're confident that we're not that far away from a tipping point where energy from solar will be competitive with fossil fuels," said Ray Kurzweil, a National Academy of Engineers panel member after the panel reported on the future of solar power in February [2008]. "I personally believe that we're within five years of that tipping point."

To do that, however, the cost of electricity produced by rooftop solar panels, for instance, will need to fall by half—from about 32 cents per kilowatt hour (kwh) today, including subsidies, to about 15 cents per kwh by 2012, according to a new report by FBR Capital Markets, an investment bank, and market researcher Solarbuzz.

A Cheaper-than-Coal Goal

Evidence of a shift appears to be taking shape around the country. Google, the Internet search company, has invested in several young solar-power start-ups with an explicit cheaper-than-coal goal. San Jose, Calif.–based Nanosolar already claims to be shipping "thin-film" solar panels that generate electricity on par with the cost of coal-fired power. And in Lexington, Mass., Frank van Mierlo and Emanuel Sachs are leading a team of engineers with one audacious mission: Make a silicon photovoltaic cell that turns sunshine into electricity as cheap as electricity from a coal-burning power plant.

"There's no doubt that we're going to see solar as cheap as coal power a lot sooner than many people realize," says Mr. van Mierlo, president of 1366 Technologies, standing beside an industrial furnace inside the company's pilot manufacturing facility.

Proof of what he says lies a few footsteps down a hallway where Sara Olibet, an applied physicist, is painstakingly measuring the efficiency of dozens of solar-cell prototypes, each with a different combination of chemical coatings designed to maximize power output.

In her lab, she uses tweezers to select one-inch-square cells and put them into a refrigerator-size machine that shines light with sun-like intensity. In addition to efficiency ratings, readings are taken along the light spectrum to evaluate the cells' coatings and other aspects being tweaked toward a single optimum formula.

For 1366 Technologies, whose name is derived from the "solar constant" of 1,366 watts per square meter that strike Earth every moment, the immediate goal is to produce a 3 percentage point gain in cell efficiency. While boosting a solar cell's efficiency from 15 percent to 18 percent may sound trivial, it would mean a huge cut in production costs, from $2.20 cents per watt today to $1 a watt—without federal or state subsidies, van Mierlo says.

At that $1-a-watt level, 1366 Technologies claims it could produce solar panels with cells delivering electricity to a home as cheaply as the delivered cost of coal power—about 10 cents per kwh.

"It's not hyperbole to say that we're within reach of grid parity," van Mierlo says. Adding to that $1 a watt a modest profit and cost of installation, the delivered cost of power would be about $3 a watt—or 18 cents per kwh—without any subsidies. At that rate, a rooftop residential solar module would produce power on par with the cost of grid power in the Northeast today.

Others are less sure. "Relative to every other significant generation source, solar is still quite expensive today," says Jim Owen, a spokesman for the Edison Electric Institute, which represents investor-owned utilities. "This technology holds significant promise, particularly utility-scale solar thermal technology. We want to tap into solar technologies and the sooner the better, but it doesn't seem around the corner."

When Grid Parity Arrives

Still, an array of experts agree that solar could cause a "disruptive" shift in US energy generation five years from now. When "grid parity" for solar arrives at that time, the nation will likely see sharp growth in solar panels installed on residential rooftops, driven not by environmental concerns, but by a desire for more economical electricity, these energy industry analysts say.

Next year [2009], enough solar panels will be sold in the US to generate 330 megawatts of power, the FBR projects. But the US could well see a 20-fold rise in US solar panel sales by 2013, enough to power about 3.5 million homes with two-kilowatt rooftop solar arrays, it says.

That surge could arrive faster with new federal tax credits that cover 30 percent of the cost of a solar installation. In some states, the news is even better for solar customers.

"The reality is that even today, there are some places in California where, with state incentives, solar already has grid parity," says Robert Margolis, senior energy analyst for the National Renewable Energy Laboratory. Nationwide, the date is closer to 2015, he says.

"Even the credit crisis, funny enough, may actually accelerate it by temporarily squelching demand and causing solar prices to come down faster," says Travis Bradford, president of the Prometheus Institute, a think tank focused on solar power.

Several analysts expect the solar panel industry to soon enter a brutal shakeout that will eliminate many weaker companies, but also benefit consumers by chopping solar panel costs in half.

Right now companies like Nanosolar that already have funding have soldiered on. Van Mierlo says 1366 is shepherding its resources. It could launch a manufacturing facility in 2010, but the company can afford to wait patiently, refining cell-manufacturing technologies until the perfect moment for full production, he says.

"In five to seven years, the idea of building a home without solar energy on it will be as silly as building without plumbing," Mr. Bradford says.

| *"Fuels produced from coal would cost around $18/barrel less to produce than crude oil–based liquids."*

Liquid Coal Is a Justifiable Alternative to Oil

Coal-to-Liquids Coalition

The Coal-to-Liquids Coalition (CTLC) is a group of the National Mining Association. In the following viewpoint, CTLC maintains that synthetic fuels from coal can break the country's dependence on foreign oil and protect the environment. With 27 percent of the world's coal reserves, the United States can use current technologies to significantly cut oil imports, protect it from unstable oil prices, create jobs, and boost its economy, the coalition claims. Furthermore, CTLC suggests that coal-based fuels burn cleaner than those derived from petroleum, with lower emissions of nitrogen oxide, carbon monoxide, and hydrocarbons.

As you read, consider the following questions:

1. What is an "import premium," as described by CTLC?

2. What types and numbers of jobs would the production of synthetic fuels require, as stated by the coalition?

3. Why are synthetic fuels more biodegradable than diesel, according to CTLC?

America's dependence on imported oil leaves our economy vulnerable to supply disruptions—and high oil prices are sending dollars overseas that are needed to create jobs here in America. It is essential that America develop a range of alternative fuel solutions to provide greater economic security and growth.

US Dependence on Oil

America's dependence on oil imports leaves the economy vulnerable to supply disruptions and price spikes, which have triggered economic downturns in the past.

- The U.S. imports 11.5 million barrels of oil per day. This represents 54 percent of the oil it consumes.

- The U.S. currently depends on foreign sources for 60 percent of its oil requirements, including crude oil and refined products. According to the Energy Information Administration (EIA), that dependence will grow to 70 percent by 2025.

- Our dependence on oil leaves our economy vulnerable to the consequences of an oil price shock, which could result from an embargo, political instability in major producing countries or terrorist attack on oil supply lines.

- In the U.S., each of the previous three oil price shocks was followed by a recession:

    The first shock led to the deep recession of 1973–75.

The second was followed by a brief recession in 1980—and eventually followed by a severe recession in 1981–82.

The Gulf War price spike was followed by a mild recession in 1990–91.

Cost of Dependence

Imported oil dependence increases America's trade deficit and weakens our economy.

- According to the National Defense Council Foundation, the economic penalties of America's oil dependence total $297.2 to $304.9 billion annually. If reflected at the gasoline pump, these "hidden costs" would raise the price of a gallon of gasoline to over $5.28. A full tank would be over $105.

- The Department of Energy estimates that each $1 billion of trade deficit costs America 27,000 jobs. Accounting for almost one-third of the total U.S. debt, oil imports are a major contributor to unemployment.

- The Southern States Energy Board estimates that if oil production peaks in 2010 and aggressive programs are not implemented to find alternative fuels, the U.S. economy will lose about US$4.6 trillion in Gross Domestic Product (GDP), 40 million job years of employment and US$1.3 billion in federal and state tax revenues.

Synthetic Fuels: A Part of the Solution

Technology has been perfected that can transform America's greatest energy resource into clean transportation fuel to reduce oil dependence.

- The U.S. has 270.7 billion tons of coal reserves. In terms of potential usable energy this is equivalent to at least twice the oil reserves of Saudi Arabia. The U.S.

has 27 percent of world coal supply—the largest of any country—but has less than 2 percent of the world's oil and less than 3 percent of its natural gas.

- With already existing technology and domestic fuels, the U.S. can reduce its oil imports by over 7.5 million barrels per day by 2025—an amount greater than all the oil we are expected to import from the entire Middle East.

- According to analysts, synthetic fuels produced from coal would cost around $18/barrel less to produce than crude oil–based liquids.

The "True Cost" of Imported Oil

There are additional, hidden costs to importing oil that are not reflected in the already high prices we pay at the pump—but have a heavy impact across the entire economy.

- "Import premium" is the estimated additional cost of every barrel of oil due to the inefficiencies of cartel pricing and oil shocks, and the military cost to insure steady access to foreign oil. The Center for Forensic Economic Studies currently estimates this "import premium" at $24/barrel of imported oil.

- The true cost of a gallon of gasoline is estimated at $5.67, once the import premium and refining costs are factored in.

- The economic loss to the U.S. when dollars are spent overseas, known as "import multiplier" must also be considered when calculating the true cost of imported oil. The Center for Forensic Economic Studies estimates that for every dollar spent on foreign crude oil, an additional $1.55 is removed from the U.S. economy.

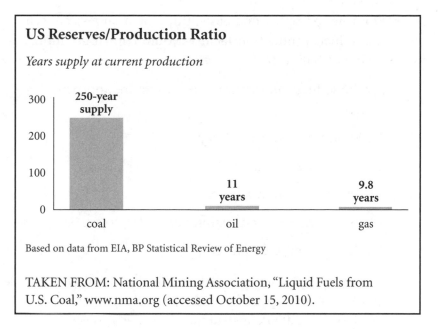

US Reserves/Production Ratio

Years supply at current production

Based on data from EIA, BP Statistical Review of Energy

TAKEN FROM: National Mining Association, "Liquid Fuels from U.S. Coal," www.nma.org (accessed October 15, 2010).

- Each $80 barrel of foreign crude oil purchased removes $124 from the U.S. economy, as a result of the negative "import multiplier."

Synthetic Fuels Will Create Jobs

Instead of sending our dollars abroad, a new synthetic fuels industry will stimulate the U.S. economy—creating quality jobs here in America.

- Spending a dollar on domestic synthetic fuels production, rather than imports, stimulates the U.S. economy and adds an additional $6.00 by generating jobs here in America.

- By replacing the 12 million barrels of oil imported daily with domestically produced synthetic fuels, the U.S. economy would reap a net benefit of $4.8 billion per day.

- On a net present value basis, building a large-scale synthetic fuels production facility would contribute more than $17 billion to U.S. GDP.

- Synthetic fuels production would require approximately:

  1,200 non-engineering designers

  640 engineers

  23,000 construction laborers

  18,000 operations and maintenance employees

  15,000 coal mine employees.

- It is estimated that each of these facilities will take 3 to 5 years to develop and 3 to 4 years to construct, creating 1,500 to 2,000 construction jobs per project.

- Permanent employment for each facility will be about 300 to 400 skilled, heavy industry workers who would receive additional benefits, such as health care and retirement plans.

Local and Regional Benefits

Local communities will not only gain quality jobs but will also gain new tax revenues and economic stimulus.

- Increased tax base directly related to the value of the project, as well as ad valorem taxes, severance taxes and royalties on coal produced.

- Major capital project/investment in the community.

- Large temporary increase in employment during construction (3–5 years).

- Permanent increase in employment of skilled operations and maintenance staff, as well as management and administrative staff.

- Increase in property tax revenues will directly benefit the schools in the community.

- Economic growth in the community related to the need for added homes, businesses and infrastructure.

- Need for research and engineering will mandate support of higher education.

- Increased tax revenues will make education infrastructure growth possible.

Synthetic Fuels and the Environment

Advanced synthetic fuels technology provides both a clean and reliable energy source for the 21st century. The emerging synthetic fuels industry is committed to developing fuels with minimal environmental impacts—with carbon capture for underground storage as an essential component of all U.S. production facilities.

Domestically produced synthetic fuels are bio-degradable, burn more cleanly than conventional diesel and meet the most stringent clean air requirements for ultra-low sulfur fuel.

Cleaner Fuels

Synthetic fuels release fewer smog-producing contaminants than regular gasoline when consumed, which can help reduce smog in our major cities.

- During gasification (the initial stage of the synthetic fuels production process), impurities in the gas stream, such as heavy metals and mercury, are easily extracted through scrubbing.

- Subsequent cleaning of the synthetic gas during the next stage of production removes substantial amounts of particulate matter and any residual metals compared to that contained in conventional petroleum-based fuels.

- The result is a near zero-sulfur fuel that offers lower emissions of nitrogen oxide, carbon monoxide and hydrocarbons.

- Consequently, synthetic fuels burn much cleaner than conventional petroleum-based fuels in use today.

- The low particulate, low mercury and almost zero sulfur emission profile of these fuels means improved human health, reduced smog, reduced tailpipe emissions, cleaner running mass transit systems in urban communities, no measurable toxic pollutants and lower emissions from fuel production.

- Synthetic fuels are also more biodegradable than conventional diesel thanks to their molecular structure and the absence of aromatics such as benzene and toluene.

Synthetic Fuel Production Plants

- The synthetic fuels production process yields virtually no measurable amounts of acids or hazardous air pollutants.

- Issues related to plant siting will be fully addressed in strict accordance with applicable requirements, including the Clean Air Act criteria governing all major plant construction and operations.

- Air emissions of conventional pollutants and mercury will be minimized in accordance with the new Clean Air Interstate Rule and a first-ever requirement for reduced mercury emissions from power plants.

Greenhouse Gas Reduction

By separating and capturing carbon dioxide during production, synthetic fuels can greatly reduce the release of greenhouse gases (GHG) into the environment.

- The gasification stage reduces the cost and energy required for carbon removal. As a result, carbon dioxide (CO_2) can be captured in a cost-effective manner for permanent storage deep below ground or in depleted oil and gas formations (through use in enhanced oil recovery).

- On a life-cycle basis, by utilizing Carbon Capture & Storage (CCS) technologies on a large-scale combined with low-GHG utility configurations, synthetic diesel derived from coal will emit fewer GHG than the imported petroleum fuels they would replace.

- Synthetic fuel is therefore consistent with existing federal policies and programs designed to lower greenhouse gas emissions—including carbon sequestration goals.

The Saudia Arabia of Coal

Coal is America's most abundant and affordable energy resource. The U.S. has been described as the "Saudi Arabia of coal," possessing the world's largest reserves—a 250-year supply—yet has only 2 percent of the world's oil.

- Using America's abundant coal resources reduces reliance on imported oil and strengthens America's energy security.

- By using available "clean coal" technologies and CCS, this valuable resource can be converted into "clean diesel" and other clean fuels without increasing the greenhouse gas profile of current petroleum-derived fuels.

- Any increased need for coal feedstocks resulting from synthetic fuels production will be mined domestically under the most comprehensive environmental and safety laws in the world.

93

> *"Coal-to-liquid . . . technologies face significant environmental and financial obstacles."*

Liquid Coal Is Not a Feasible Alternative to Oil

PRWeb Newswire

In the following viewpoint, a report details how coal-to-liquid (CTL) and oil shale technologies face major financial and environmental obstacles. According to the Energy Information Administration, coal-to-oil production is projected to rise to 91 million barrels per year by 2035. Despite this projection, oil shale and CTL production face many environmental constraints, such as the need for large amounts of water and large carbon emissions. Ultimately, the report asks investors of these technologies to give careful thought to the potential risks involved in these oil alternative productions. PRWeb Newswire is a leader in online news distribution.

As you read, consider the following questions:

1. According to New York state comptroller Thomas DiNapoli, as cited by the author, what do investors need before they can fully assess the benefits of coal-to-liquid projects?

2. What are some of the companies involved in coal-to-liquid (CTL) development, according to PRWeb Newswire?

3. According to studies cited by the author, when is CTL viable as a fuel?

As pressure mounts to develop unconventional fuel sources to enhance U.S. energy security, a new Ceres report released today shows that coal-to-liquid (CTL) and oil shale technologies face significant environmental and financial obstacles—from water constraints, to technological uncertainties to regulatory and market risks—that pose substantial financial risks for investors involved in such projects. . . .

"There are costs that go along with the benefits of extracting and exploiting these unconventional fuel sources," said New York State Comptroller Thomas DiNapoli. "Before investors can fully assess the benefits of developing oil shale and liquefied coal projects, we need full disclosure of the environmental, regulatory and technological risks surrounding these unproven reserves. Every investor has to take a strong look at these risks."

Developing Unconventional Fuel Sources

An increased focus on energy security and dwindling petroleum reserves are driving development of unconventional liquid fuel sources in the U.S. The Obama Administration's recent extension of the offshore oil-drilling moratorium through 2011 has also renewed investor interest in on-shore oil reserves. . . .

CTL production is projected to rise in the U.S. from virtually no production today to about 91 million barrels per year by 2035, according to the Energy Information Administration. Major companies involved in CTL development include Shell, Rentech, Baard and DKRW.

Relative Carbon Intensity of Fossil Fuels	
Fossil Fuel	CO_2 Emitted per Unit of Energy
Natural gas (best)	1.0
Crude oil	1.4
US coal	1.8
Liquid coal (worst)	2.5

TAKEN FROM: Steven Stoft, *Carbonomics: How to Fix the Climate and Charge It to OPEC*. Nantucket, MA: Diamond Press, 2008.

"Investors with holdings in companies involved in coal-to-liquids and oil shale projects should ask these companies to open their books and explain their strategies for managing these risky projects," said Mindy Lubber, president of Ceres and director of the $9 trillion Investor Network on Climate Risk. "The energy- and water-intensive nature of both coal-to-liquids and oil shale, combined with technological uncertainties and state and federal requirements for low carbon fuels spell diminishing returns for investors."

The Energy Independence and Security Act of 2007 prohibits federal agencies including the Department of Defense and the Air Force from procuring alternative or synthetic fuels, unless contract provisions stipulate that life-cycle greenhouse gas emissions do not exceed equivalent conventional fuel emissions produced from conventional petroleum sources.

"We are leery of investing in oil shale and coal-to-liquids and have turned down specific opportunities to invest in CTL developers in the past," said Steven Heim, Managing Director and Director of ESG Research and Shareholder Engagement, Boston Common Asset Management, LLC. "The energy resource seems promising but huge obstacles may be regional water scarcity and the lack of large-scale carbon capture and sequestration infrastructure."

The Report's Key Findings

Water constraints: Oil shale and CTL development may be constrained by each technology's need for large amounts of water. Oil shale production requires 1.5 to 5 barrels of water for every barrel produced while CTL requires 5 to 7 barrels of water for every barrel of produce produced. Water constraints are especially problematic for oil shale production, because the reserves are located in the water-stressed states of Colorado, Wyoming and Utah.

Regulatory Risks: Current and potential regulations seeking to limit carbon dioxide emissions such as low carbon fuel standards and lifecycle emissions requirements pose potentially serious risks to carbon-intensive oil shale and CTL. EPA's [Environmental Protection Agency's] proposed Tailoring Rule regulating GHG emissions from new sources will also likely apply to CTL facilities.

Core Technological Uncertainty: Oil shale technology is still in the early stages of development, particularly processes that involve heating the oil shale in place and extracting it from the ground. CTL technologies are further along but combining the various technologies into a commercially viable plan still faces operational and technical challenges.

Carbon Capture and Sequestration (CCS) Uncertainty: Given their carbon intensity, oil shale and CTL will be dependent on CCS if they are to survive as low carbon fuel standards and other carbon-reducing regulations take hold. CCS still faces great uncertainly, however, regarding its commercial viability, public financing levels, enabling policies and potential markets for captured CO_2.

Market Risks: The economic competitiveness of oil shale and CTL is contingent on high oil prices. Studies show that CTL is viable as a fuel when the price of oil exceeds \$40–55 a barrel. Oil shale may not be profitable unless oil prices are in the \$70–95 per barrel range. Neither of these estimates takes into account potential carbon prices, or CCS costs, which are very expensive and would raise the price-per-barrel competitiveness level.

The report calls on investors to give careful thought to these wide-ranging risks and engage with oil companies, CTL developers and end-users such as airlines to further understand the risks that companies are assuming.

Periodical Bibliography

The following articles have been selected to supplement the diverse views presented in this chapter.

Kevin Bullis   "Mixing Solar with Coal to Cut Costs," *Technology Review*, September 4, 2009.

Shamsul Ghani   "Coal: A Potential Alternate to Oil and Gas," *Pakistan & Gulf Economist*, December 5, 2010.

Kari Hawkins   "Flying Skies with Coal Mix Fuel," *Redstone (AL) Rocket*, July 30, 2010.

Ed Hiserodt   "Coal in Your Car's Tank," *New American*, June 9, 2008.

Ralph Hostetter   "Coal Liquefaction for Alternative Fuel?," *Newsmax*, August 6, 2008.

Martin La Monica   "Making Solar Cheaper than Coal," *CNET News*, March 6, 2009.

Keith Lieberthal   "Liquid Coal a Slippery Business," *TheStreet*, June 21, 2007.

Andrew Moseman   "How Solar Power Can Become Cheaper than Coal," *Discover*, July/August 2010.

Ted Nace   "Which Has a Bigger Footprint, a Coal Plant or a Solar Farm?," *Grist*, November 17, 2010.

Frank O'Donnell   "The Return of Nazi Oil," www.tompaine.com, July 19, 2006.

Science Daily   "Wind, Water, and Sun Beat Biofuels, Nuclear, and Coal," December 11, 2008.

OPPOSING
VIEWPOINTS®
SERIES

CHAPTER 3

Should Coal Use
Be Phased Out?

Chapter Preface

Mountaintop removal is a method of strip mining in which the summit or summit ridge of a mountain is blown away with explosives to extract coal seams. Beforehand, the area is deforested and cleared of vegetation and topsoil. When mining is completed, the debris from the removal, or overburden, is either stacked onto the mountain to mimic its original contours or relocated to nearby valleys. Mountaintop removal primarily is practiced in the Appalachian Mountains and in other parts of the eastern United States, mainly Kentucky and West Virginia. The method supplies an estimated 5 percent of the nation's coal burned for electricity.

Calling for a moratorium on this method, some opponents argue that overburden dumped into valleys disrupts and pollutes natural water systems. "Coal companies have buried a staggering 2,000 miles of freshwater streams in Appalachia in order to mine coal," contends Appalachian Voices, a nonprofit activist group. "Coal sludge, a toxic byproduct of separating coal from other rock, is held in massive impoundments held back by unregulated dams, and leaking endangers local water tables and community drinking water,"[1] the group adds. Others point out that the ancient Appalachians are in danger of being obliterated. "Indeed, it is utterly inconceivable that the Smokies would be blasted, the Rockies razed, the Sierra Nevadas flattened—that bombs the equivalent to Hiroshima would be detonated every single week for the past three decades," asserts actress Ashley Judd, who traces her ancestry to the region and works with the Alliance for Appalachia to Stop Mountaintop Removal. "The fact that the Appalachians are the Appalachians makes this environmental genocide possible and permissible,"[2] she notes.

1. Appalachian Voices, "Water," http://appvoices.org/water/.
2. Ashley Judd, "My Old Kentucky Home: Threatened by Mountaintop Removal," *OnEarth* Community Blog, July 6, 2010. www.onearth.org/community-blog/my-old-kentucky-home-threatened-by-mountaintop-removal.

But supporters insist that mountaintop removal is beneficial to local communities and to the nation at large. "Mountain top development brings many things to communities, such as golf courses, airports, and sports complexes. It stimulates the economy in those regions and creates more jobs," states Tyler Phipps, an agricultural economics student at the University of Kentucky. He adds, "From a national perspective, you can see how America avoids being dependent on foreign countries for energy."[3] In the following chapter, the authors deliberate the regulations and bans proposed for the coal industry and energy use as part of the debate on whether coal use should be phased out.

---

3. Tyler Phipps, "'Mountain Top Development' Benefits Ky.," letter to the editor, *Kentucky Kernel*, October 25, 2010. http://kykernel.com/2010/10/25/letter-to-the-editor-mountain-top-development-benefits-ky/.

VIEWPOINT

| "Federal policy should . . . prevent the construction of any new coal plant unless it employs [carbon capture and storage]."

New Coal Power Plants Without CCS Should Be Banned

Barbara Freese, Steve Clemmer, and Alan Nogee

Barbara Freese is the author of Coal: A Human History. *Steve Clemmer is research director for the Union of Concerned Scientists Clean Energy Program, of which Alan Nogee is director. In the following viewpoint, the authors argue that the construction of new coal plants will lock in dangerously high emissions for decades. The authors claim that the existing plants are old and inefficient, and most proposed plants will not have the most advanced clean-coal technology. Moreover, Freese, Clemmer, and Nogee state that the future retrofitting of plants built today will ultimately result in major cost and energy penalties. The authors advocate prohibiting new plants without carbon capture and storage technology, replacing coal with cleaner energy sources and enforcing stricter emissions standards.*

As you read, consider the following questions:

1. What is Freese, Clemmer, and Nogee's position on building a new coal plant to replace an older one?

2. Why are the authors skeptical that US coal plants will adopt CCS technologies in the future?

3. According to the authors, what happened after the widespread coal-plant construction in the 1960s and 1970s?

While we need additional information to decide how much to invest in coal plants that capture CO_2, it is already clear that further investments in new coal plants that do *not* capture CO_2 would be a mistake. Federal policy should therefore prevent the construction of any new coal plant unless it employs CCS [carbon capture and storage]. . . .

New Coal Plants Still Release CO_2

Virtually all the new coal plants that have been proposed will, just like their predecessors, release 100 percent of the CO_2 they produce into the atmosphere, where it will linger—and contribute to global warming—throughout this century and into the next. Advocates of new coal plants frequently argue that new plants emit less CO_2 than old ones and may be seen as a "step in the right direction." However, this argument assumes that we can take far more time to make the needed emissions reductions than we can actually afford.

No one can argue the fact that the existing U.S. coal fleet is old and inefficient; the average age of each plant is over 35 years, and the average efficiency is roughly 33 percent. In other words, for every three tons of coal a plant burns, one ton is converted into electricity while two tons are lost as waste heat. The third of the coal fleet built before 1970 has even lower efficiency—averaging only 28 percent—and higher emissions.

In terms of efficiency, new IGCC [integrated gasification combined cycle] plants are expected to average about 38 percent. The efficiency of new pulverized coal plants varies depending on type: less advanced subcritical units have efficiencies of only 33 to 37 percent, more advanced supercritical units have efficiencies of 37 to 40 percent, and the most advanced ultrasupercritical units (operating in Europe and Japan) have operating efficiencies above 40 percent.

Remarkably, only 17 of the proposed pulverized coal plants would use supercritical technology, while 40 would use the least-efficient subcritical technology. Twenty-four proposed plants would use subcritical circulating fluidized bed (CFB) technology; these plants potentially represent a greater climate threat than pulverized coal plants because they produce much higher levels of heat-trapping nitrous oxide.

Even if the proposed plants were all substantially more efficient than today's plants, that would not reduce CO_2 emissions by a single ton unless the newer plants actually replace older ones—which is not intended for most of the proposed plants. In the states that require power producers to show that a new coal plant is needed before it can be built (many states do not), producers generally claim the new plants are needed to meet growing electricity demand. In the absence of policy changes, this would be consistent with the Energy Information Administration's (EIA's) 2008 projection of a dramatically expanded U.S. coal fleet by 2030: 100 gigawatts (GW) of new coal plant construction and the retirement of only 3.9 GW of older plants.

One reason why the newly proposed plants are so costly is that they often require the construction of new power lines, coal delivery or handling facilities, and cooling water systems—all costs that could be avoided if these projects were actually designed as replacement plants rather than additions to the fleet. In short, these new coal plants would each emit millions of tons of additional CO_2 during a time when we need to dramatically reduce such emissions.

Moreover, even if a new coal plant did replace an older one, it would still represent a costly, long-term commitment to an energy technology with substantially higher CO_2 emissions than any non-coal option. New coal plants are extraordinarily expensive (construction costs have risen 30 to 80 percent since 2004), take years to build (most proposed plants would not begin operating until 2013 or later), and require decades of operation to return the massive capital investment. Locking in such high emissions for so long cannot be reconciled with the sustained emissions cuts we must achieve to avoid the worst consequences of global warming. And, as we discuss below, these new plants are simply not necessary given the cleaner options available to us.

A Dangerous Strategy

[An] MIT [Massachusetts Institute of Technology] report . . . shows that the cost and energy penalties associated with adding CCS technology to a coal plant (which are considerable even when the technology is incorporated into the plant's original design) increase substantially for a plant that was not designed to accommodate it.

This is a particular problem for pulverized coal plants (the great majority of the 114 proposed plants discussed above). The process of capturing CO_2 diverts a large amount of steam from the boiler that would otherwise have been used by the steam turbine to generate power. As a result, the boiler runs at full capacity but the turbine runs well below its most efficient rate. This steam loss "unbalances the rest of the plant so severely," in MIT's words, that the result is an even greater loss of efficiency. Instead of losing 25 to 28 percent of its maximum potential power, as a plant outfitted with CCS at the start would, a plant retrofitted with CCS would lose 36 to 41 percent of its power. This suggests that the cost of energy from the retrofitted plant would rise by considerably more than the 59 percent increase associated with a new plant already equipped with CCS. As a result, the MIT report concludes that, "retrofits are unlikely."

While the retrofit penalty for IGCC plants is expected to be less than for pulverized coal, certain fundamental design features such as the gasifier and gasifier configuration must change if carbon is to be captured. If, for example, the IGCC plant is built with the wrong kind of gasifier, the plant could lose far more of its power when CCS is added than if it had chosen another type of gasifier with CCS in mind. Cost estimates for retrofitting an IGCC plant with CCS are remarkably scarce; the MIT report concluded that there was insufficient information to evaluate most of the available configurations quantitatively.

Another important consideration is the proximity of the plant to an appropriate sequestration site. Many plants have been proposed in locations far from the geologic formations that could store their CO_2; these plants would face considerably higher CO_2 transportation costs (generally by pipeline) than plants in more suitable locations.

Moreover, given the fact that many U.S. coal plant operators have fiercely resisted installing pollution controls for sulfur dioxide (SO_2 "scrubbers"), their assurances that CCS will be added at some future date must be viewed with skepticism. Even though SO_2 scrubbers have been available since the 1980s, only a third of U.S. coal plants have them, and their costs (though relatively high) are likely to pale in comparison to the cost of adding CO_2 capture to a coal plant built without it—especially a pulverized coal plant.

Finally, the failure of a plant's backers to include the cost of a future CCS retrofit in the plant's price tag prevents regulators, ratepayers, and investors from knowing its true cost. It would also be impossible to judge how the proposed plant compares with cleaner energy alternatives.

A Financial and Environmental Mistake

The fact that so many coal plants have been proposed does not mean they are actually needed to meet U.S. electricity demand. The last time U.S. utilities engaged in a massive campaign to build base-load power plants (i.e., plants designed to operate nearly continuously) was in the late 1960s and 1970s, when the utilities greatly overestimated demand growth and greatly underestimated construction costs (particularly of nuclear plants). The results were often financially disastrous: utilities cancelled 184 proposed power plants, including 80 nuclear plants and 84 coal plants, just in the period from 1974 through 1978. In other cases costly coal plants were built years before they were needed. Under traditional regulation, the power sector is typically allowed to recover all plant construction costs from ratepayers, including an administratively determined return on investment. This gives utilities a financial incentive to build plants whether they are needed or not, and to resist changing course even when circumstances warrant it.

Fortunately, there are commercially available options for avoiding and reducing emissions from coal plants by either reducing electricity demand or substituting low-carbon fuels for coal. Demand can be reduced while meeting energy needs by improving the efficiency with which electricity is produced, transmitted, and consumed. Lower-carbon alternatives to coal include natural gas, renewable resources such as wind, solar, geothermal, bioenergy, and hydropower, and potentially nuclear energy.

Energy efficiency improvements have enormous potential to reduce emissions at a low cost. In addition, our analyses (and those of others) have shown that non-hydroelectric renewable energy supplies in the United States could be increased from about 2.5 percent of electricity use today to 20 or even 25 percent by 2020 or 2025—offsetting much of the projected growth in power plant carbon emissions—without raising consumer energy costs (and in some cases perhaps slightly lowering costs).

Most power producers prevented from building coal plants without CCS will find that their customers' energy needs are better met through increased conservation and efficiency and/or expanded renewable electricity generation. In some cases, additional natural gas generation may also be warranted.

At the same time, states that have adopted new or stricter renewable electricity standards (which require power producers to obtain a specific percentage of their electricity from renewable resources) and energy efficiency standards have found that their once-perceived need for additional coal-fired power has been dramatically reduced. At least 60 coal plant proposals were cancelled, abandoned, or rejected by regulators in 2007, illustrating just how weak the need for such plants is. The DOE's [Department of Energy's] list of proposed coal projects, which included 151 as recently as May 2007, had shrunk to 114 by February 2008.

Increasingly aggressive state efficiency and renewable electricity standards combined with expected federal legislation will further reduce the need to consider new coal plants, buying additional time for CCS technology—and non-coal alternatives—to develop. . . . Several large-scale CCS projects are scheduled to become operational in the 2012–2015 range—not much later than the many proposed coal plants without CCS would come into service (2013 or later), though conclusive proof that CO_2 has been safely sequestered would require additional time.

One of the consequences of the current rush to construct coal plants is that many projects are experiencing substantial delays in construction due to shortages of equipment, materials, and specialized labor. The question before the United States is not, therefore, what kind of new coal plants should meet our needs today, because any coal plant will take years to construct. The question is what kind of new coal plants—if any—should meet our needs in the middle of the next decade and beyond, during a period when we need to achieve dramatic emissions reductions.

CCS may or may not prove safe and cost-effective, but there is no justifiable argument for building new coal plants without it. In the event CCS is shown to be unsafe or too costly, the act of building new coal plants will have locked us into decades of higher CO_2 emissions and the much more difficult and costly challenge of reducing emissions by replacing these plants with cleaner alternatives. If, on the other hand, CCS is shown to be a viable solution, coal plants built with the technology will enable us to pursue emissions reductions far more cost-effectively than plants that would have to be retrofitted with CCS.

Clearly, as long as there is no financial penalty for emitting CO_2 and no requirement for new coal plants to be built with carbon capture, power producers have a strong economic disincentive to build such plants. As a result, while a number of coal projects involving CCS have been announced, many appear unlikely to proceed without a change in U.S. climate policy. Barring the construction of coal plants without CCS would greatly accelerate the speed at which the technology is developed, and bring us closer to having the necessary information to determine whether it is something we can and should widely deploy.

However, such a policy alone would do nothing to reduce emissions from existing plants, and a policy that sets a high bar for new plants would create an incentive to keep older, inefficient plants operating longer. A requirement that new coal plants capture CO_2 must therefore be combined with policies that drive emissions reductions in the existing fleet. At the very least these policies should include a system for putting a price on carbon emissions, such as a cap-and-trade program.

The Cost of Coal Power

- The approximate annual damage burden of coal combustion in power plants ... is roughly £355.75 billion [$465.32 billion].

- the approximate global damage burden related to accidents in the coal power chain ... is £161.28 million [$223.52 million].

- the approximate annual damage costs of mining ... is £674 million [$934.20 million].

Greenpeace,
"The True Cost of Coal," November 26, 2008.

A Strong Performance Standard

One promising policy mechanism for preventing the construction of new coal plants without CCS is a CO_2 performance standard, which imposes a limit on how much CO_2 a new coal plant could emit per megawatt-hour (MWh). Such standards have already been adopted in both California and Washington State and proposed in several bills before the 110th Congress [in 2007–2008]. A federal standard at least as strict as California's and Washington's should be enacted and immediately applied to all coal plants commencing construction in the next five years; a more stringent standard should be applied to plants commencing construction after that time.

The current California standard requires that all new baseload power plants emit CO_2 at a rate no higher than combined-cycle natural gas plants. Though the best new combined-cycle plants may emit as little as 800 lb. of CO_2 per MWh, the California Public Utilities Commission set the state standard at 1,100 lb. per MWh to reflect the higher emissions rates of some existing combined-cycle plants. Washington followed suit.

Four federal proposals would also establish performance standards linked to the performance of natural gas plants. Two would limit emissions at the same level as California (one permanently and one as an interim measure); the other two, because they would be modeled specifically on the performance of new combined-cycle plants, would be somewhat stricter than California's standard. . . .

Since new coal plants would be intended to operate well into the carbon-constrained century ahead, it is not unreasonable to require them to emit less CO_2 than a natural gas plant. Setting a performance standard based on what the given control technology can achieve rather than the performance of a competing energy source is a cornerstone principle embodied in the federal Clean Air Act New Source Review and New Source Performance Standards. And as the price of CCS technology gradually falls, it may even be reasonable to require it at new natural gas plants as well as coal plants. CCS is already being investigated at gas plants in Europe.

Any CO_2 performance standard must be paired with a strong cap-and-trade policy. Because the performance standard would only apply to new plants and does nothing to reduce emissions from existing plants, a cap-and-trade program that applies to both new and existing plants would ensure that overall emissions are reduced. By the same token, a cap-and-trade program is no substitute for a performance standard. While such a program would discourage the construction of some of the new coal plants that have been proposed, existing flaws in the energy markets (such as the possibility that the cost of future CO_2 allowances may be passed through to ratepayers) make a performance standard necessary to avoid locking the United States in to decades of high emissions from new coal plants already in the pipeline.

Construction Recommendations

The United States should prevent the construction of coal plants that do not employ CCS technology by pursuing the following policies:

- Enact a CO_2 performance standard that requires plants commencing construction between now and 2013 to add CCS to their full emissions stream and achieve a CO_2 emissions rate of 1,100 lb. per MWh or lower.

- Enact a stricter standard that requires plants commencing construction *after* 2013 to meet an emissions limit that reflects maximum achievable capture rates (currently estimated to be 80 to 90 percent on a MWh basis).

"If we're going to ban new coal plants, we might as well raise the carbon bar for everyone."

A Ban on New Coal Power Plants May Be Counterproductive

Part I: Jackie Grom, Part II: Jeffrey Rubin

Jackie Grom is a writer based in Canada. Jeffrey Rubin is a former chief economist at CIBC World Markets and author of Why Your World Is About to Get a Whole Lot Smaller. *In the following viewpoint, Grom and Rubin oppose a ban on new coal power plants. In Part I, Grom contends that researchers modeled four energy scenarios—taking into account renewables and increased energy efficiency—and found that the price of natural gas would skyrocket and carbon emissions would not be significantly reduced if a ban were imposed. In Part II, Rubin states that a ban on new coal plants increases the cost of energy, which burdens domestic manufacturers and gives foreign competitors powered by cheap coal an economic advantage. Instead, Rubin proposes a charge for emissions and a carbon tariff on imports.*

As you read, consider the following questions:

1. What four energy scenarios did the researchers model, as described by Grom?

2. As told by Grom, how would the demand for natural gas increase in the United States if wind power is chosen?

3. What does saying "no" to coal plants actually mean, in Rubin's opinion?

What would happen if the United States stopped building coal-fired power plants? The solution may not be the panacea some have predicted. Although the plants are the single biggest polluter in the United States, contributing to smog, acid rain, and global warming, a new analysis shows that banning them would increase the cost of natural gas while doing little to aggressively combat climate change.

Coal has faced strong opposition from policymakers and the public. In 2007, 59 out of 151 proposed U.S. coal plants were either denied licenses by state governments or abandoned, while environmental groups contested dozens in court. What's more, the governors of at least two states, Florida and Kansas, have said that they will not approve new coal-fired power plants.

But energy researchers Jay Apt and Adam Newcomer of Carnegie Mellon University in Pittsburgh, Pennsylvania, wondered if banning these plants would do any good. To find out, they modeled four different energy scenarios through the year 2030. One scenario takes a business-as-usual approach, with no ban on coal plants, keeps energy demand growth at historical rates, and new demand met by the current contribution of energy providers, including coal, nuclear power, natural gas, oil, and renewables. The next three scenarios ban the construction of future coal-fired power plants. In two of these, energy demand still grows at historical rates, but one scenario meets demand with increases in natural gas production, while the other assumes a large push for wind energy, supplemented by natural gas. The final scenario quenches increased energy needs with wind and natural gas as well, but it assumes that U.S. residents won't require any more energy than they do today—if, say, people become much more efficient in their energy usage; the only increase in demand would come from a growing population. The team applied the model to three main regions in the United States: the Midwest, Texas, and parts of the East Coast.

In every model, the use of natural gas skyrocketed, the researchers report online this week in *Environmental Science & Technology*. Under the wind scenario, for example, natural gas demand rose 55% by 2030 in Texas, 430% on the East Coast, and 470% in the Midwest. As demand for natural gas doubles, it can lead to anywhere from a 175% to 500% increase in price, says Apt. That could drive companies that rely on natural gas overseas, he says, especially those that aren't tied to working in the United States.

The researchers also found that carbon dioxide emissions didn't drop as much as they had expected. If coal plants are not banned, by 2030 emissions rise 43% in Texas, 24% in parts of the East Coast, and 17% in the Midwest, according to the model. But if they are banned, by 2030, emissions are cut anywhere from 6% to 15% in Texas, 18% to 48% along parts of the East Coast, and 10% to 27% in the Midwest. Overall, that's not enough to meet target emission reductions, says Apt. To avoid more than 2°C warming—and the deadly heat waves, intense droughts, and sea level rise it would bring—the United States needs to cut emissions about 80% by 2050. Only the scenario that assumes no increase in energy demand comes close to meeting this standard—and just on the East Coast.

Howard Herzog, an energy researcher at the Massachusetts Institute of Technology in Cambridge, says that a better approach would be to keep coal as part of the energy portfolio, but to find new ways to curb CO_2 emissions from these plants. "Singling out any one fuel" is a bad idea, he says. Instead, "we need to look at technologies [such as carbon capture and storage] that allow us to reduce our carbon emission and still utilize our most important domestic supply [of energy]."

Part II

Just because the Waxman-Markey bill [H.R. 2454, the American Clean Energy and Security Act of 2009, also known as the cap-and-trade bill] is roadkill on the Senate floor doesn't mean the U.S. doesn't already pay a heavy price for its carbon emissions. If you doubt that, try getting your local power utility to build a new coal-fired generating station. Between 2006 and 2009, applications for 83 new coal plants were either turned down or withdrawn in the U.S.

Coal is still abundant across North America, but outside of a few coal states and the province of Alberta, no one dares build new coal-fired generating plants these days. Coal's carbon emissions have made it a pariah fuel, at least in this part of the world. And with good reason: coal emits twice as much carbon per unit of energy as natural gas does.

Of course, when we say no to new coal plants, we're not really saying no to more power generation. Instead, we're saying, "Let's burn natural gas or, even better, use renewables like wind to generate power, often at double or more the cost of coal." (Falling natural gas prices have only recently made it cost-competitive with coal.) And we're passing those costs along to our own steel and auto-assembly plants.

Unfortunately their competitors overseas are run on the cheap coal-fired power North American plants are increasingly denied. China may lead the world in the production of wind turbines, but eighty per cent of that country's power comes from burning coal.

More Harm than Good

I don't know about you, but it seems to me we've got our carbon policy ass-backwards. We handicap our industries by forcing them to use more expensive, greener power while they have to compete with imports that are created with much cheaper coal-fired power. And all the while we pretend that we are protecting our economy from crippling carbon costs that would diminish our competitiveness.

But ironically we do the economy more harm than good by not charging for emissions at the same time as we force power users to pay that much more for coal alternatives.

You shouldn't make domestic industries pay twice. If they are going to fork out more for using less carbon-emitting power, you shouldn't make them do it again by losing market share to imports that don't have to pay for their own emissions.

Wouldn't it be better to put an actual price on emissions instead of just de facto banning new coal plants? By pricing domestic carbon emissions, we could then apply that same cost to imports through a carbon tariff and thereby achieve a level playing field. Instead, by pretending we don't price carbon when really we do, we saddle our producers with higher energy costs but deny them any commercial benefit from using greener power, which they would get from a carbon tariff.

The status quo is a lose-lose proposition. If we're going to ban new coal plants, we might as well raise the carbon bar for everyone.

> *"When our nation establishes a health-driven energy policy, one that replaces our dependence on coal with clean, safe alternatives, we will prevent the deterioration of global public health."*

Reducing Coal Use Would Promote Public Health

Alan H. Lockwood, Kristen Welker-Hood, Molly Rauch, and Barbara Gottlieb

Alan H. Lockwood is a past president of Physicians for Social Responsibility (PSR) and neurology and nuclear medicine professor at the University at Buffalo, New York. A nurse and environmental health scientist, Kristen Welker-Hood is the program director at PSR's Environment & Health Program, of which Molly Rauch is senior policy analyst and Barbara Gottlieb is program deputy director. In the following viewpoint, the authors maintain that coal pollutants pose major threats to human health. The stages in coal's lifecycle—mining, transportation, washing, combustion, and disposal—are linked to heart disease, cancer, stroke, and respiratory diseases, the authors maintain. Additionally, global warming conditions as a result of coal use, they insist, threaten lives and impact the quality of the air and water. Therefore, the authors offer several policy recommendations: reducing carbon dioxide emissions, placing caps on pollution, prohibiting construction of new coal-burning power plants, and increasing the nation's capacity to produce clean, renewable energy.

As you read, consider the following questions:

1. What risks and dangers do coal miners face, as stated by the authors?

2. How do the authors link coal pollutants with the genetic basis of asthma?

3. How does global warming already affect human health, as described in the viewpoint?

Coal pollutants affect all major body organ systems and contribute to four of the five leading causes of mortality in the U.S.: heart disease, cancer, stroke, and chronic lower respiratory diseases. This conclusion emerges from our reassessment of the widely recognized health threats from coal. Each step of the coal lifecycle—mining, transportation, washing, combustion, and disposing of post-combustion wastes—impacts human health. Coal combustion in particular contributes to diseases affecting large portions of the U.S. population, including asthma, lung cancer, heart disease, and stroke, compounding the major public health challenges of our time. It interferes with lung development, increases the risk of heart attacks, and compromises intellectual capacity.

Oxidative stress and inflammation are indicated as possible mechanisms in the exacerbation and development of many of the diseases under review. In addition, the report addresses another, less widely recognized health threat from coal: the contribution of coal combustion to global warming, and the current and predicted health effects of global warming.

The Life Cycle of Coal

Electricity provides many health benefits worldwide and is a significant contributor to economic development, a higher standard of living, and an increased life expectancy. But burning coal to generate electricity harms human health and compounds many of the major public health problems facing the industrialized world. Detrimental health effects are associated with every aspect of coal's life cycle, including mining, hauling, preparation at the power plant, combustion, and the disposal of post-combustion wastes. In addition, the discharge of carbon dioxide into the atmosphere associated with burning coal is a major contributor to global warming and its adverse effects on health worldwide.

Coal mining leads U.S. industries in fatal injuries and is associated with chronic health problems among miners, such as black lung disease, which causes permanent scarring of the lung tissues. In addition to the miners themselves, communities near coal mines may be adversely affected by mining operations due to the effects of blasting, the collapse of abandoned mines, and the dispersal of dust from coal trucks. Surface mining also destroys forests and groundcover, leading to flood-related injury and mortality, as well as soil erosion and the contamination of water supplies. Mountaintop removal mining involves blasting down to the level of the coal seam—often hundreds of feet below the surface—and depositing the resulting rubble in adjoining valleys. This surface mining technique, used widely across southern Appalachia, damages freshwater aquatic ecosystems and the surrounding environment by burying streams and headwaters.

After removal of coal from a mine, threats to public health persist. When mines are abandoned, rainwater reacts with exposed rock to cause the oxidation of metal sulfide minerals. This reaction releases iron, aluminum, cadmium, and copper into the surrounding water system and can contaminate drinking water.

Coal washing, which removes soil and rock impurities before coal is transported to power plants, uses polymer chemicals and large quantities of water and creates a liquid waste called slurry. Slurry ponds can leak or fail, leading to injury and death, and slurry injected underground into old mine shafts can release arsenic, barium, lead, and manganese into nearby wells, contaminating local water supplies. Once coal is mined and washed, it must be transported to power plants. Railroad engines and trucks together release over 600,000 tons of nitrogen oxide and 50,000 tons of particulate matter into the air every year in the process of hauling coal, largely through diesel exhaust. Coal trains and trucks also release coal dust into the air, exposing nearby communities to dust inhalation. The storage of post-combustion wastes from coal plants also threatens human health. There are 584 coal ash dump sites in the U.S., and toxic residues have migrated into water supplies and threatened human health at dozens of these sites.

The combustion phase of coal's lifecycle exacts the greatest toll on human health. Coal combustion releases a combination of toxic chemicals into the environment and contributes significantly to global warming. Coal combustion releases sulfur dioxide, particulate matter (PM), nitrogen oxides, mercury, and dozens of other substances known to be hazardous to human health. Coal combustion contributes to smog through the release of oxides of nitrogen, which react with volatile organic compounds in the presence of sunlight to produce ground-level ozone, the primary ingredient in smog. . . .

These health effects damage the respiratory, cardiovascular, and nervous systems and contribute to four of the top five leading causes of death in the U.S.: heart disease, cancer, stroke, and chronic lower respiratory diseases. Although it is difficult to ascertain the proportion of this disease burden that is attributable to coal pollutants, even very modest contributions to these major causes of death are likely to have large effects at the population level, given high incidence rates. Coal combustion is also responsible for more than 30% of total U.S. carbon dioxide pollution, contributing significantly to global warming and its associated health impacts.

Respiratory Effects of Coal Pollution

Pollutants produced by coal combustion act on the respiratory system to cause a variety of adverse health effects. Air pollutants—among them nitrous oxide (NO_2) and very small particles, known as $PM_{2.5}$—adversely affect lung development, reducing forced expiratory volume (FEV) among children. This reduction of FEV, an indication of lung function, often precedes the subsequent development of other pulmonary diseases.

Air pollution triggers attacks of asthma, a respiratory disease affecting more than 9% of all children in the U.S. Children are particularly susceptible to the development of pollution-related asthma attacks. This may be due to their distinct breathing patterns, as well as how much time they spend outside. It may also be due to the immaturity of their enzyme and immune systems, which assist in detoxifying pollutants, combined with incomplete pulmonary development. These factors appear to act in concert to make children highly susceptible to airborne pollutants such as those emitted by coal-fired power plants.

Asthma exacerbations have been linked specifically to exposure to ozone, a gas produced when NO_2 reacts with volatile organic compounds in the presence of sunlight and heat. The risk to children of experiencing ozone-related asthma exacerbations is greatest among those with severe asthma. That risk exists even when ambient ozone levels fall within the limits set by the EPA [Environmental Protection Agency] to protect public health.

Coal pollutants trigger asthma attacks in combination with individual genetic characteristics. This gene-environment interaction means that some individuals are more susceptible to the respiratory health effects of coal pollution. The genetic polymorphisms that appear to make people more susceptible include those that control inflammation and those that deal with oxidative stress, or the presence of highly reactive molecules, known as free radicals, in cells.

Coal pollutants play a role in the development of chronic obstructive pulmonary disease (COPD), a lung disease characterized by permanent narrowing of airways. Coal pollutants may also cause COPD exacerbations, in part through an immunologic response—i.e., inflammation. PM exposure disposes the development of inflammation on the cellular level, which in turn can lead to exacerbations of COPD. COPD is the fourth leading cause of mortality in the U.S.

Exposures to ozone and PM are also correlated with the development of and mortality from lung cancer, the leading cancer killer in both men and women.

Cardiovascular Effects of Coal Pollution

Pollutants produced by coal combustion damage the cardiovascular system. Coronary heart disease (CHD) is a leading cause of death in U.S., and air pollution is known to negatively impact cardiovascular health. The mechanisms by which air pollution causes cardiovascular disease have not been definitively identified but are thought to be the same as those for respiratory disease: pulmonary inflammation and oxidative stress. Studies in both animals and humans support this theory, showing that pollutants produced by coal combustion lead to cardiovascular disease, such as arterial occlusion (artery blockages, leading to heart attacks) and infarct formation (tissue death due to oxygen deprivation, leading to permanent heart damage).

Recent research suggests that nitrogen oxides and $PM_{2.5}$, along with other pollutants, are associated with hospital admissions for potentially fatal cardiac rhythm disturbances. The concentration of $PM_{2.5}$ in ambient air also increases the probability of hospital admission for acute myocardial infarction, as well as admissions for ischemic heart diseases, disturbances of heart rhythm, and congestive heart failure. Additionally, cities with high NO_2 concentrations had death rates four times higher than those with low NO_2 concentrations. These studies show important immediate effects of coal pollutants on indicators of acute cardiovascular illness.

There are cardiovascular effects from long-term exposure as well. Exposure to chronic air pollution over many years increases cardiovascular mortality. This relationship remains significant even while controlling for other risk factors, such as smoking. Conversely, long-term improvements in air pollution reduce mortality rates. Reductions in $PM_{2.5}$ concentration in 51 metropolitan areas were correlated with significant increases in life expectancy, suggesting that air quality improvements mandated by the Clean Air Act have measurably improved the health of the U.S. population. Reducing exposure to the pollutants emitted by coal combustion is therefore an important aspect of improving cardiovascular health for the population at large.

Nervous System Effects of Coal Pollution

In addition to the respiratory and cardiovascular systems, the nervous system is also a target for coal pollution's health effects. The same mechanisms that are thought to mediate the effect of air pollutants on coronary arteries also apply to the arteries that nourish the brain. These include stimulation of the inflammatory response and oxidative stress, which in turn can lead to stroke and other cerebral vascular disease.

Several studies have shown a correlation between coal-related air pollutants and stroke. In Medicare patients, ambient levels of $PM_{2.5}$ have been correlated with hospital admission rates for cerebrovascular disease, and PM_{10} has been correlated with hospital admission for ischemic stroke.

(Eighty-seven percent of all strokes are ischemic.) $PM_{2.5}$ has also been associated with an increase in the risk of—and death from—a cerebrovascular event among post-menopausal women. Even though a relatively small portion of all strokes appear to be related to the ambient concentration of PM, the fact that nearly 800,000 people in the U.S. have a stroke each year makes even a small increase in risk a health impact of great importance.

Coal pollutants also act on the nervous system to cause loss of intellectual capacity, primarily through mercury. Coal contains trace amounts of mercury that, when burned, enter the environment. Mercury increases in concentration as it travels up the food chain, reaching high levels in large predatory fish. Humans, in turn, are exposed to coal-related mercury primarily through fish consumption. Coal-fired power plants are responsible for approximately one-third of all mercury emissions attributable to human activity.

A nationwide study of blood samples in 1999–2000 showed that 15.7% of women of childbearing age have blood mercury levels that would cause them to give birth to children with mercury levels exceeding the EPA's maximum acceptable dose for mercury. This dose was established to limit the number of children with mercury-related neurological and developmental impairments. Researchers have estimated that between 317,000 and 631,000 children are born in the U.S. each year with blood mercury levels high enough to impair performance on neurodevelopmental tests and cause lifelong loss of intelligence.

Global Warming and Coal Pollution

Coal damages the respiratory, cardiovascular, and nervous systems through pollutants acting directly on the body. But coal combustion also has indirect health effects, through its contribution to greenhouse gas emissions. Global warming is already negatively impacting public health and is predicted to

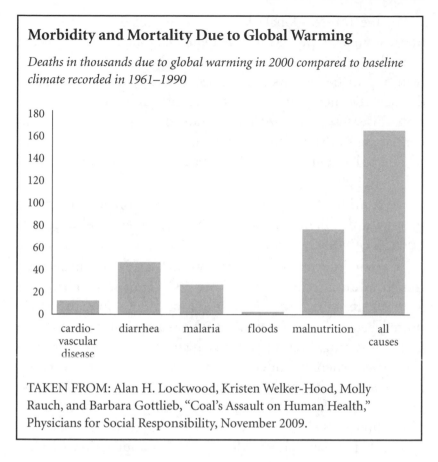

Morbidity and Mortality Due to Global Warming

Deaths in thousands due to global warming in 2000 compared to baseline climate recorded in 1961–1990

TAKEN FROM: Alan H. Lockwood, Kristen Welker-Hood, Molly Rauch, and Barbara Gottlieb, "Coal's Assault on Human Health," Physicians for Social Responsibility, November 2009.

have widespread and severe health consequences in the future. Because coal-fired power plants account for more than one third of CO_2 emissions in the U.S., coal is a major contributor to the predicted health impacts of global warming. The effects of global warming already in evidence include increases in global average land and ocean surface temperatures; increases in snow melt and receding glaciers; increases in the mean sea level; and changes in precipitation. These global climate changes are already affecting human health. The World Health Organization estimated global warming to be responsible for 166,000 deaths in 2000, due to additional mortality from malaria, malnutrition, diarrhea, and drowning.

In the future, global warming is expected to continue to harm human health. More frequent heat waves are projected to lead to a rise in heat exhaustion and heat stroke, potentially resulting in death, especially among elderly and poor urban dwellers. Declining air and water quality, an increase in infectious diseases, and a shrinking food supply are expected to contribute to disease and malnutrition, increase the migration of affected populations, and increase armed conflict and global instability. . . .

A continued reliance on coal combustion for electricity production will contribute to the predicted health consequences of global warming.

Carbon capture and sequestration (CCS) has been promoted as an effective way to keep CO_2 emissions out of the atmosphere, but substantial research and development are required before it can be used on the scale needed to mitigate global warming. Even then, the danger remains that CCS storage areas, whether underground or under the ocean, could leak, negating the value of CO_2 capture and storage. CCS also incurs other threats to health, including the danger of asphyxiation in the case of a large-scale CO_2 leak and the acidification of ocean waters. Moreover, the application of CCS would require continued coal mining, transportation, combustion, and waste storage, thus prolonging the emission of coal's toxic pollutants that harm human health.

Policy Recommendations

The U.S. is at a crossroads for determining its future energy policy. While the U.S. relies heavily on coal for its energy needs, the health consequences of that reliance are multiple and have widespread and damaging impact. Coal combustion contributes to diseases already affecting large portions of the U.S. population, including asthma, heart disease, and stroke, thus compounding the major public health challenges of our time. Coal combustion also releases significant amounts of carbon dioxide into the atmosphere. Unless we address coal, the U.S. will be unable to achieve the reductions in carbon emissions necessary to stave off the worst health impacts of global warming. Based on that assessment, [Physicians for Social Responsibility] finds it essential to translate our concern for human health into recommendations for public policy.

> Emissions of carbon dioxide should be cut as deeply and as swiftly as possible, with the objective of reducing CO_2 levels to 350 parts per million, through two simultaneous strategies:

- Strong climate and energy legislation that establishes hard caps on global warming pollution coming from coal plants.

- The Clean Air Act (CAA). Carbon dioxide and other greenhouse gas emissions from coal plants have been designated pollutants under the CAA. The EPA should be fully empowered to regulate carbon dioxide under the CAA so that coal's contribution to global warming can be brought to an end.

- There should be no new construction of coal-fired power plants, so as to avoid increasing health-endangering emissions of carbon dioxide, as well as criteria pollutants and hazardous air pollutants.

- The U.S. should dramatically reduce fossil fuel power plant emissions of sulfur dioxide and nitrogen oxides so that all localities are in attainment for national ambient air quality standards.

- The EPA should establish a standard, based on Maximum Achievable Control Technology, for mercury and other hazardous air pollutant emissions from electrical generation.

- The nation must develop its capacity to generate electricity from clean, safe, renewable sources so that existing coal-fired power plants may be phased out without eliminating jobs or compromising the nation's ability to meet its energy needs. In place of investment in coal (including subsidies for the extraction and combustion of coal and for capture of carbon and other pollutants), the U.S. should fund energy efficiency, conservation measures, and clean, safe, renewable energy sources such as wind energy, solar, and wave power.

These steps comprise a medically defensible energy policy: one that takes into account the public health impacts of coal while meeting our need for energy. When our nation establishes a health-driven energy policy, one that replaces our dependence on coal with clean, safe alternatives, we will prevent the deterioration of global public health caused by global warming while reaping the rewards in improvements to respiratory, cardiovascular, and neurological health.

| *"Mining and burning coal is a socially responsible component of sound energy policy."*

Reducing Coal Use Would Be Socially Irresponsible

Paul K. Driessen

Paul K. Driessen is senior policy adviser for the Committee for a Constructive Tomorrow (CFACT) and the Congress of Racial Equality (CORE) as well as author of Eco-Imperialism: Green Power—Black Death. *In the following viewpoint, Driessen asserts that restricting coal would harm nations, communities, and families. While the author supports renewable energy and conservation, he says that solar and wind power is still expensive and unreliable, unable to provide the electricity necessary for acceptable living standards. Indeed, Driessen charges environmental activists with stopping new coal power plants and the use of coal as transportation fuel, leaving America dependent on foreign oil and vulnerable to energy shortages.*

As you read, consider the following questions:

1. How does the author defend power companies?

Paul K. Driessen, "The Social Responsibility of Coal: Relying More on Coal Generates Benefits That Are Too Often Ignored," *The Progressive Conservative*, September 3, 2008. Copyright © 2008 Paul K. Driessen, Senior Policy Advisor, Congress of Racial Equality (CORE) and Committee for a Constructive Tomorrow (CFACT). Reprinted by permission.

2. What does "hard green" social responsibility ignore, in Driessen's view?

3. What are Driessen's arguments against global warming?

They get little credit for their efforts, but most resource extraction, manufacturing, and power generation companies strive to be "socially responsible"—by emphasizing energy efficiency, resource conservation, pollution control, and worker safety in producing the raw materials, consumer products, and electricity that improve, safeguard, and enrich our lives.

It's not easy, due to the nature of their business, public intolerance for any ecological impacts, and the fact that "corporate social responsibility" [CSR] is often defined and used by radical Leftist and environmentalist activist groups to promote ideological agendas. Above all, activists want to engineer a "wholesale transformation" of our energy and economic system, away from hydrocarbon fuels and into "eco-friendly" renewable resources; reduce our living standards to "sustainable" levels (their definition again); and give them control over the power that sustains our modern society.

This hardcore Leftist and Green version of CSR largely ignores socio-economic considerations, the many benefits of fossil fuel and nuclear power, the significant land and environmental impacts of wind and solar power and the production and use of ethanol as a motor fuel, as well as the oppressive effects of soaring energy prices on jobs and poor families.

Energy Economics 101

Speaker Nancy Pelosi closed down the U.S. House of Representatives on August 1, 2008, to avoid an energy vote that Democrats would have lost, and later displayed her acumen on the subject when she opined: "natural gas is a clean, cheap alternative to fossil fuels." News flash: Natural gas is a fossil fuel.

An Energy Economics 101 course is clearly needed, so that members of both major political parties can legislate more astutely, understand why mining and burning coal is a socially responsible component of sound energy policy, and help stanch the unnecessary flow of $700 billion a year in foreign oil payments.

Energy is the master resource, the foundation for everything we eat, use, and do. Sound policies ensure that energy is abundant, reliable, and affordable. Restricting supplies in the face of rising global demand drives up prices and sends shockwaves through families, industries, communities, and nations.

Average total energy costs for a typical American household doubled from $2,400 in 1997 to over $5,000 in 2007. Food prices also soared, while wages remained stagnant. More low and middle income families have been forced to choose between heating, eating, driving, medicines and rent, with little left over for vacations, emergencies, retirement, college, or charity.

Thankfully, most electricity bills rose more modestly, because half of all U.S. electricity is generated using coal, and the price for that fossil fuel has risen far less than oil, gasoline, and natural gas prices. However, in places like Florida, where coal is verboten, natural gas is promoted but drilling for it is banned, and wind and solar are all the rage, electricity prices continue to climb. Florida Power & Light Company must pay four times as much for photovoltaic power as for coal power, the Heartland Institute reports, and schools face budget crunches for buses and electricity.

Speculative Risks

America has centuries' worth of coal. Our reliance on this resource has tripled since 1970, but sulfur dioxide and particulate emissions are down 40% and 90% below 1970 levels, respectively, notes air pollution expert Joel Schwartz. New technologies and regulations will reduce coal power plant emissions even further by 2020, but even current emissions (including mercury) pose no significant risks to human health, he emphasizes.

Radical environmentalists worry and wail about speculative health risks, to justify anti-coal campaigns. But their concerns often disappear when the discussion shifts to millions of Africans who die every year from real, preventable lung and intestinal diseases that result from an absence of electricity for cooking, heating, refrigeration, safe drinking water, hospitals and decent living standards. Wind and solar will save few of those lives—and, yet, Green pressure groups stridently oppose fossil fuel, nuclear, and hydroelectric power for Africa.

U.S. electricity consumption will continue climbing, even with conservation, because our population and technology use are increasing steadily. Meanwhile, 59 coal-fired plants were cancelled in 2007, thanks to eco-activists, who are challenging 50 more.

No Excess Capacity

The U.S.A. now has virtually no excess capacity, and switching to natural gas as a primary power plant fuel (and fuel for backup generators to support wind farms) means electricity prices could increase "as much as tenfold," says energy analyst Mark Mills, especially if we continue to ban drilling. "After that we may see forced conservation, or even blackouts in rotation among business and residential customers."

Energy shortages and price hikes could cost millions of jobs in the automotive, airline, tourism, food and beverage, textiles, paper making, plastics, chemicals, metals, and manufacturing industries—especially if Congress also enacts cap-and-trade rules. Most will never be replaced by "Green collar" jobs that some claim will be created by intermittent, unreliable wind and solar energy.

Switching to plug-in hybrid cars will only exacerbate the problem. They will need a well-stocked power grid to plug into, and current energy policies virtually ensure that it won't be there.

In addition to balance of trade issues, over-reliance on imports has major national security implications, as Russia's invasion of Georgia [Gruzia] forcefully reminded Europe. Germany imports 40% of its natural gas from Russia, and six Eastern European countries are entirely dependent on [Russian president Vladimir] Putin's energy. Shackled further by their opposition to nuclear power, fear of climate change Armageddon and fixation on the Kyoto Protocols [international agreement that sets targets for reducing greenhouse gas emissions], the European Union has barely protested actions by a rogue bear that has already cut off natural gas supplies to Latvia, Lithuania and the Czech Republic, to impose its will.

That should cause Congress to reflect more soberly on U.S. dependence on oil from Venezuela, Nigeria, Iran, and Russia. Coal could be converted into synthetic liquid and gas fuels, to replace the oil and gas we refuse to develop, but legal and regulatory hurdles restrict that option, too.

No Convincing Evidence

A key justification for these anti-energy policies is cataclysmic global warming. However, 32,000 scientists have signed the Oregon Petition, saying they see "no convincing evidence" that humans are causing climate change, or that it will be catastrophic. Climate models continue to predict chaos but, as one scientist wryly notes, faith in their predictions is as misplaced as reliance on emails from Nigeria advising recipients that they have won the Lotto.

Global temperatures have not increased since 1998, despite steadily increasing carbon dioxide levels, and solar scientists like Pal Brekke say the sun's formerly high activity level is leveling off or abating, which could bring falling global temperatures.

China and India are planning or building 700 coal-fired power plants; European countries plan to build 50 more in five years, to reduce dependence on Russian gas; and other nations are also increasing fossil fuel use for transportation and power generation.

Thus, no matter how much the U.S.A. reduces its energy use, driving, heating, air-conditioning and living standards—no matter how much it punishes poor families or commits economic suicide—its actions would not reduce global CO_2 levels, or affect the Earth's climate.

We need to conserve and continue improving renewable energy technologies that currently provide just 0.5% of our energy. But, at this time, renewables are simply too inefficient, expensive, and unreliable to permit a shutdown of hydrocarbon-based systems.

Putting "social responsibility" and "environmental justice" in the hands of eco-activists and Liberal Democrats is like giving a machine gun to an idiot child. We need definitions that recognize the full spectrum of societal needs, and energy policies that acknowledge life in the real world.

> "For the United States, this bulb switch would facilitate shutting down 80 coal-fired plants."

Using Compact Fluorescent Bulbs Instead of Incandescents Will Decrease Coal Use

Lester R. Brown

Lester R. Brown is founder of the Earth Policy Institute in Washington, DC, and author of many books, including Plan B 4.0: Mobilizing to Save Civilization. *In the following viewpoint, Brown advocates the phase-out of incandescent lightbulbs and the increased use of compact fluorescents to reduce coal consumption and carbon emissions. Measures taken to end the sale of incandescents in Australia, the United Kingdom, New Zealand, and several US states can allow the closing of dozens of coal plants, he states. This simple step, Brown argues, can decrease electricity consumption by 3 percent and more globally, which is important as the world faces the consequences of climate change.*

As you read, consider the following questions:

1. What is the energy savings of a 24-watt compact fluorescent bulb over its lifetime, as described by Brown?

2. What are the cost savings of a compact fluorescent bulb,
   as illustrated by the author?

3. How does the author address the concern of mercury in
   fluorescent bulbs?

On February 20, 2007, Australia announced it would phase
out the sale of inefficient incandescent light bulbs by
2010, replacing them with highly efficient compact fluorescent
bulbs that use one fourth as much electricity. If the rest of the
world joins Australia in this simple step to sharply cut carbon
emissions, the worldwide drop in electricity use would permit
the closing of more than 270 coal-fired (500 megawatt) power
plants. For the United States, this bulb switch would, facilitate
shutting down 80 coal-fired plants.

A Tipping Point

The good news is that the world may be approaching a social
tipping point in this shift to efficient light bulbs. On April 25,
2007, just two months after Australia's announcement, the Canadian government announced it would phase out sales of incandescents by 2012. Mounting concerns about climate change
are driving the bulb replacement movement.

In mid-March, a U.S. coalition of environmental groups—
including the Natural Resources Defense Council, the Alliance
to Save Energy, the American Coalition for an Energy-Efficient
Economy, and the Earth Day Network—along with Philips
Lighting launched an initiative to shift to the more-efficient
bulbs in all of the country's estimated 4 billion sockets by
2016.

In California, the most populous state, Assemblyman Lloyd
Levine is proposing that his state phase out the sale of incan-

descent light bulbs by 2012, four years ahead of the coalition's deadline. Levine calls his proposed law the "How Many Legislators Does It Take to Change a Light Bulb Act." On the East Coast, the New Jersey legislature is on the verge of requiring state government buildings to replace all incandescent bulbs with compact fluorescents by 2010 as part of a broader statewide effort to promote the shift to more-efficient lighting. . . .

The European Union [EU], now numbering 27 countries, announced in March 2007 that it plans to cut carbon emissions by 20 percent by 2020. Part of this cut will be achieved by replacing incandescent bulbs with compact fluorescents. In the United Kingdom, a nongovernmental group called Ban the Bulb has been vigorously pushing for a ban on incandescents since early 2006. Further east, Moscow is urging residents to switch to compact fluorescents. In New Zealand, Climate Change Minister, David Parker, has announced that his country may take similar measures to those adopted by Australia.

In April [2007], Greenpeace urged the government of India to ban incandescents in order to cut carbon emissions. Since roughly 640 million of the 650 million bulbs sold each year in this fast-growing economy are incandescents, the potential for cutting carbon emissions, reducing air pollution, and saving consumers money is huge.

At the industry level, Philips, the world's largest lighting manufacturer, has announced plans to discontinue marketing incandescents in Europe and the United States by 2016. More broadly, the European Lamp Companies Federation (the bulb manufacturers' trade association) is supporting a rise in EU lighting efficiency standards that would lead to a phase-out of incandescent bulbs.

At the commercial level, Wal-Mart, the world's largest retailer, announced a marketing campaign in November 2006 to boost its sales of compact fluorescents to 100 million by the end of 2007, more than doubling its annual sales. In the U.K.,

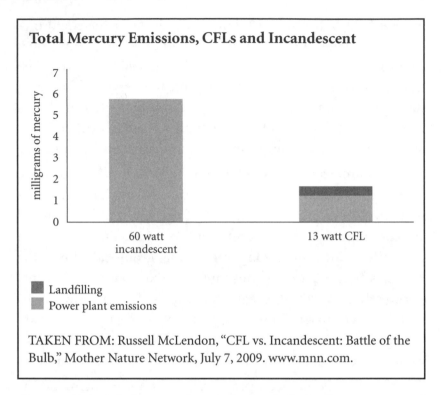

Total Mercury Emissions, CFLs and Incandescent

TAKEN FROM: Russell McLendon, "CFL vs. Incandescent: Battle of the Bulb," Mother Nature Network, July 7, 2009. www.mnn.com.

Currys, Britain's largest electrical retail chain, has announced that it will discontinue selling incandescent light bulbs.

Immediate Gains in Energy Efficiency

Switching light bulbs is an easy way of realizing large immediate gains in energy efficiency. A study for the U.S. government calculated that the gasoline equivalent of the energy saved over the lifetime of one 24 watt compact fluorescent bulb is sufficient to drive a Prius from New York to San Francisco. While a worldwide phase out of the inefficient incandescents would reduce world electricity use by more than 3 percent, shifting to more-efficient street lighting and replacing older fluorescent tubes with newer, more-efficient ones might double this reduction in power use.

Although highly efficient compact fluorescent bulbs have been around for a generation, they have until recently been on the fringe, used only by environmentally-minded consumers and typically sold in hardware stores, but not in supermarkets. One reason consumers lacked interest was that the new bulbs can cost five times as much as incandescents. Only the more knowledgeable consumers knew that a compact fluorescent bulb uses only one fourth as much electricity as an incandescent bulb, lasts 10 times as long, and easily saves $50 during its lifetime.

One disadvantage of compact fluorescents is that each bulb contains a small amount of mercury, roughly one fifth the amount in a watch battery. This mercury is only a small fraction of that released into the atmosphere by the additional coal burned to power an incandescent.

Mercury released by coal-fired power plants is the principal reason why 44 of the 50 states in the United States have issued mercury intake advisories limiting the consumption of fish from freshwater streams and lakes. Nonetheless, worn-out compact fluorescents, watch batteries, and other items that contain mercury still need to be recycled properly. Fortunately, this is possible, whereas the mercury spewing from coal smokestacks blankets the countryside, ending up in the water and food supply.

Shifting to the highly efficient bulbs sharply reduces monthly electricity bills and cuts carbon emissions, since each standard (13 watt) compact fluorescent over its lifetime reduces coal use by more than 210 pounds. Such a shift also substantially reduces air pollution, making it obviously attractive for fast-growing economies plagued with bad air like China and India.

In the United States, an ingenious website called 18sec onds.org (the name derives from the time it takes to change a light bulb), provides a running tally of compact fluorescents sold nationwide since January 1, 2007. As of early May [2007], it totaled nearly 37 million bulbs, yielding a reduction in carbon emissions comparable to taking 260,000 cars off the road.

Sponsored by Yahoo! and Nielsen, the site also provides data on how many dollars are being saved and how much less coal is burned. Data are available on the website for each state, providing a convenient way of monitoring local progress in replacing incandescents.

The Challenge for Each of Us

The challenge for each of us, of course, is to shift to compact fluorescents in our own homes if we have not already. But far more important, we need to contact our elected representatives at the city, provincial, or state level and at the national level to introduce legislation to raise lighting efficiency standards, in effect phasing out inefficient incandescent light bulbs. Few things can cut carbon emissions faster than this simple step.

In a world facing almost daily new evidence of global warming and its consequences, there is a need for a quick decisive victory in the effort to cut carbon emissions and stabilize climate. If we can engineer a rapid phase-out of incandescent light bulbs it would provide just such a victory, generating momentum for even greater advances in climate stabilization.

"We need safe inventions first before we
ban incandescent light bulbs."

Compact Fluorescent Bulbs Are Hazardous to Health and the Environment

Rosalind Peterson

Rosalind Peterson is a retired US Department of Agriculture Farm Service Agency crop loss adjustor. In the following viewpoint, Peterson claims that compact fluorescent bulbs can be dangerous and that incandescents should not be phased out. Unbeknownst to most consumers, she contends, broken fluorescents can cause serious skin and eye injury as well as mercury contamination in homes, the air, soil, and water supplies if not properly recycled and disposed of. And Peterson suggests that the shift to fluorescent lighting will put highly polluting plants in operation and may not cut mercury emissions even if coal-generated power is reduced.

As you read, consider the following questions:

1. How do fluorescent bulbs harm people in the workplace, in Peterson's opinion?

2. As described by the author, what facts about cleaning broken bulbs containing mercury do most consumers not know?

3. How are fluorescent bulbs unsafe to use, as pointed out by Peterson?

There is a movement by many states and localities to ban incandescent light bulbs and convert to total use of fluorescent bulbs (CFL) to save energy. And yet there are few who have read the small print on the tiny inside package label of fluorescent bulbs or heard about the EPA's [Environmental Protection Agency's] problems with regard to mercury contamination. What should you know about fluorescent light bulbs?

Eight Things to Know

1) Heat resistant glass is used in these bulbs. The quartz arc tube, when operating creates light by generating a considerable amount of ultraviolet (UV) radiation. How much exposure to this UV radiation goes through the heat resistant glass and what are the human health problems associated with this exposure? How does the public know that the exposure is safe for children and adults?

2) If the glass is broken serious skin burn and eye inflammation from short-wave ultraviolet radiation may occur. Many of these fluorescent bulbs are constructed without automatic shut offs if the light bulbs are broken, thus exposing people to this type of harmful UV radiation.

3) In the workplace many employees subjected to this type of lighting develop eyestrain and headaches. In many cases the flickering of these types of lights causes workplace eyestrain and irritation from the lighting being too bright. These issues do not appear to have any solutions at this time other than the use of incandescent light bulbs.

4) According to California Assembly Bill 1109 (2007) Section (e): "Most fluorescent lighting products contain hazardous levels of mercury. Most incandescent lighting products contain hazardous levels of lead. California prohibits disposing of hazardous lighting products in the solid waste stream. The hazardous materials in these products can be managed through recycling, but current recycling opportunities and levels are virtually nonexistent for most consumers . . ." Fluorescent light bulbs contain both mercury and lead.

5) According to California Assembly Bill 1109 (2007) Section (f): "Fluorescent lighting products delivering the same level of light at the same level of efficiency can have widely varying levels of mercury . . ." It appears that the product labels do not designate the levels of mercury in their products so that consumers can pick the ones with the lowest level of mercury to use and for toxic waste disposal.

6) Whether or not shifting from incandescent lighting to fluorescent light will result in a net reduction of mercury emissions due to the displacement of coal fired electricity generation is questionable at this time. More highly polluting production plants using mercury will need to be put online making fluorescent bulbs to replace incandescent bulbs. In addition, the lack of recycling will put this mercury into landfills where it will leach into drinking water sources and contaminate landfills as is the case at the present time.

7) Clean up instructions for mercury broken bulbs are not provided on the outside of fluorescent manufacturer's packaging at this time. Therefore, consumers are not aware of the following EPA facts:

A. "Never use a vacuum cleaner to clean up mercury. The vacuum will put mercury into the air and increase exposure. The vacuum appliance will be contaminated and have to be disposed of in a hazard waste disposal site."

B. "Never use a broom to clean up mercury . . ."

C. "Never wash mercury contaminated items in a washing machine. Mercury may contaminate the machine and/or pollute sewage."

D. Everyone should be removed from the area where the spill occurred; this includes pets. The impacted areas should be sealed off from other areas and all ventilation systems should be turned off from the impacted area.

E. "Never walk around as your shoes might be contaminated with mercury. Contaminated clothing can spread mercury around." In case of fire the entire area will be contaminated with mercury and should be sealed off from any type of use.

F. "If a spill occurs on carpet, curtains, upholstery or other like surfaces, these contaminated items should be thrown away in accordance . . ." and with assistance of your local hazard waste disposal site.

8) The outside label on most fluorescent light bulbs does not carry this hazard information leading the public to believe that these bulbs are safe and that they do not need special recycling as hazardous wastes. And the outside label does not let you know that used bulbs should be placed in containers where they can't be broken prior to disposal.

[In] an article written by Joseph Farah, in WorldNetDaily, on April 16, 2007, is the following statement: ". . . but with limited recycling prospects and the problems experienced . . . some think the government, the green community, and industry are putting the cart before the horse . . ." when they ferociously market fluorescent light bulbs. According to this article one local citizen in Prospect, Maine has to raise $2,000 to have an environmental cleanup firm do the work and her homeowners insurance won't cover the cost.

Solutions to Fluorescents Are Years Away

Now we have [former] Vice-President Al Gore with books, movies, and speeches promoting the use of fluorescent light

A Rash of Health Problems

There has been a 'rash' of health problems associated with exposure to electromagnetic radiation such as that emitted by CFLs [compact fluorescent lightbulbs]. In Sweden, according to polls, up to 290,000 people, or more than 3% of the population, have reported suffering symptoms of EHS [electrohypersensitivity] when exposed to electromagnetic radiation. Symptoms range from joint stiffness, chronic fatigue, headaches, tinnitus, respiratory, gastric, skin, sleep and memory problems, to depressive tendencies, Alzheimer's disease and all classes of cancer.

Walt McGinnis, Oilcrash.com.

bulbs knowing fully well that they are not safe. Some do catch fire if not used in the proper lighting fixtures, which do not include, for example, track, recessed or dimmer fixtures. (Many packages are not clearly marked on this subject.) And known solutions to the problems associated with fluorescent light bulbs are five to ten years away. And prior to any ban on incandescent light bulbs there should be collection and disposal sites available everywhere for these types of products.

Americans also want built-in protections from mercury contamination for air, soil and water supplies prior to any mass changeover to this type of light bulb. Why are these types of light bulbs being promoted when they may not be safe for consumers to use and dispose of when broken?

New lighting systems could be found that work better than either incandescent or fluorescent bulbs. Technological inventions could reduce the amount of electricity used by incandescent bulbs and a whole new generation of lighting systems could be put online like LED lights which may or may not be proven safe with regards to public health. With recycling about ten years away industry could be working on mercury free fluorescent lighting systems to meet energy reduction requirements. We need safe inventions first before we ban incandescent light bulbs.

The EPA warns everyone that ". . . mercury has long been known to have toxic effects on human and wildlife . . . Mercury is a toxic, persistent, bioaccumulative pollutant that affects the nervous system . . . As it moves through the environmental media, mercury undergoes a series of complex chemical and physical transformations . . ." Local, state, and federal agencies should be working to reduce the amount of mercury in the environment, not promoting more usage of this highly toxic chemical. No one currently knows how many fluorescent bulbs are in landfills at this time. If we expand their usage we are adding to a monumental mercury pollution problem. We definitely need recycling before we need to use more of these fluorescent light bulbs.

Where are thousands of these fluorescent bulbs, made from (a polluting industry), going to be recycled in the future if we ban incandescent bulbs? Are there recycling centers that can handle mercury contamination from these types of bulbs and take care of clean up when these bulbs are broken in your home and in landfills where they may be dumped? The public has many questions and few answers. Contact your elected representatives and find out where they stand on this important issue. Vote no on legislation that would ban incandescent light bulbs in California and other states. We can have safe and energy efficient light bulbs in the future if we work toward those goals today.

Periodical Bibliography

The following articles have been selected to supplement the diverse views presented in this chapter.

Neela Banerjee — "Taking on a Coal Mining Practice as a Matter of Faith," *New York Times*, October 28, 2006.

Lester R. Brown — "Coal-Fired Power on the Way Out?," www.ipsnews.net, February 24, 2010.

Shirley Stewart Burns — "Mountaintop Removal in Central Appalachia," *Southern Spaces*, September 30, 2009.

Joseph Farah — "Consumers in Dark over Risks of New Light Bulbs," *WorldNetDaily*, April 16, 2007.

Joshua Frank — "Calling for a Coal Moratorium," www.socialistworker.org, May 8, 2009.

Rick Held — "Mountaintop Removal," *Metro Pulse*, February 28, 2008.

John McQuaid — "Mining the Mountains," *Smithsonian*, January 2009.

Luminous Maximus — "Ban the Bulb?," *American Thinker*, April 3, 2007.

Steven Mufson — "Midwest Has 'Coal Rush,' Seeing No Alternative," *Washington Post*, March 10, 2007.

Janet Pelley — "Coal Ban Could Heat up Electricity Prices," *Environmental Science & Technology*, May 13, 2009.

Nancy L. Reinhart — "Coal-Burning Power a Public Health Issue," *Nation's Health*, November 2009.

Ron Rosenbaum — "In Defense of Incandescence," *Slate*, January 30, 2008.

 CHAPTER 4

Is Coal Mining Safe?

Chapter Preface

On April 5, 2010, America's worst mining disaster in forty years hit the Upper Big Branch mine, operated by Massey Energy in Birchton, West Virginia. Twenty-nine people died as a result of an explosion, caused by high levels of methane gas, in the mine. "You're gonna hit methane," said Kevin Lambert, who was about to start his shift at the mine. "You don't know where it comes from, 'cause it could come from a crack, could come [from] anywhere. All it takes is a spark,"[1] he said.

Following the explosion, an administrator with the Mine Safety and Health Administration (MSHA) reported that twenty-five workers had died and four were missing, and the rescue mission began that evening. Two safety chambers within Upper Big Branch were stocked with enough air, food, water, and other supplies to sustain twelve miners for ninety-six hours, or four days. The next afternoon, rescuers had to leave the mine due to dangerous amounts of methane and carbon dioxide, as they prepared to drill three one-thousand-foot-long shafts to release the gases. On April 7, eleven of the dead were retrieved. The last of the bodies were recovered two days later, including four that rescuers had not seen amid the terrible conditions of the mine. None of the miners had reached the safety chambers.

Because of the deadly gases in the Upper Big Branch mine, teams from the MSHA and West Virginia Office of Miners' Health, Safety, and Training delayed inspections for more than two months. As of December 2010, officials have suggested that a mantrip—a shuttle train or car that transports miners

---

1. Quoted in CBS News video, April 7, 2010, www.cbsnews.com/video/watch/?id=6371152n.

to and from work areas—set off the spark that caused the explosion. Civil and criminal investigations were still pending at the time of this writing.

The Upper Big Branch tragedy thrust coal-mine safety back into public scrutiny. The last major mining disaster, an explosion at another West Virginia mine, killed twelve people in 2006. In the following chapter, the authors examine the legislation, policies, and technologies that are enforced or proposed to ensure the safety of mines and protect miners in the event of an accident.

| "H.R. 5663, the Miner Safety and Health Act, will fix . . . problems that have allowed some mine owners to operate on the margins of safety without being held accountable."

Stricter Regulation Can Improve the Safety of Coal Mines

George Miller

George Miller is a US representative from California and chairman of the House Education and Labor Committee and Democratic Policy Committee. In the following viewpoint, Miller argues that preventable accidents and deaths expose the weaknesses in the nation's mine safety laws. Legislation is urgently needed, he maintains, to increase oversight of mine operators that flout safety precautions and the concerns of employees. The author declares that, if enacted, the Miner Safety and Health Act will break the pattern of violations among the most perilous coal mines and hold operators accountable.

George Miller, "Chairman Miller Statement at Committee Hearing on H.R. 5663, the Miner Safety and Health Act," The United States House of Representatives: Committee on Education and Labor, July 13, 2010. Reproduced by permission.

As you read, consider the following questions:

1. In the author's words, what claims did miners in Beckley, West Virginia, make against a mining company?

2. How would the Miner Safety and Health Act deal with violation appeals, as described by Miller?

3. What does the Miner Safety and Health Act recognize about employers' reactions to whistleblowers, in Miller's view?

We meet today to consider urgent legislation to address serious flaws in our nation's mine safety laws.

These flaws became devastatingly obvious on April 5th [2010] when a massive explosion ripped through Upper Big Branch Mine in West Virginia, killing 29 miners.

It is simply unacceptable for mine workers to die or be injured in preventable accidents.

It is unacceptable for mine companies to game the mine laws to avoid protecting their employees.

It is unacceptable that mine workers across the nation live in fear of their jobs if they raise safety issues at work.

And it is unacceptable that mine workers are not given the most updated safety technology and training to protect their health and safety.

While it will take months to determine the precise cause of the Upper Big Branch explosion, we already understand the disastrous results when a mine owner operates on the margins of safety in order to put more coal on the belt.

Further study and investigation isn't needed to understand the result when workers' voices are silenced by fear of retaliation for speaking out on safety problems.

And, we know the consequences for safety when an operator repeatedly disregarded safety and does everything to avoid tougher oversight.

Miners die.

A Pattern of Noncompliance

This message was clear when we travelled to Beckley, West Virginia to hear from miners and families of miners who lost loved ones on April 5th.

The testimony was chilling. What we heard was how an outlaw mine company valued production over the lives of human beings.

We heard how miners would get sick because there wasn't enough oxygen.

We heard how widespread fear and intimidation has paralyzed miners from demanding [that] management fix serious problems.

And, we learned how a federal agency lacked the resources and legal authority to fix these chronic problems.

In 2009, Massey's Upper Big Branch mine was cited 515 times for serious violations, including 54 orders to evacuate the mine due to urgent safety concerns.

While the mine corrected unsafe conditions when confronted by MSHA [Mine Safety and Health Administration] inspectors, it repeatedly slipped back into a pattern of noncompliance.

In the weeks before the explosion, MSHA closed the mine seven times, six times for failures related to improper mine ventilation.

Despite this pattern of serious violations, there was little MSHA could do to get Massey to turn this operation around.

The millions of dollars in proposed fines over the years didn't work.

Dozens of temporary closure orders didn't work.

And, it seems, complaints that miners were not getting enough air below didn't work either.

The Upper Big Branch mine is the perfect example of how current law is inadequate, especially for those operations that do everything to flout the law.

H.R. 5663, the Miner Safety and Health Act, will fix these problems that have allowed some mine owners to operate on the margins of safety without being held accountable. [As of May 2011, the act had not been brought before the U.S. House of Representatives for a vote.]

Among other provisions, the legislation will revamp the broken 'pattern of violations' sanctions so that our nation's most dangerous mine operations are able to improve safety quickly.

Furthermore, responding to serious concerns raised in Beckley, the Miner Safety and Health Act will empower workers to speak up about safety concerns, strengthening whistle-blower protections.

The bill will eliminate incentives for owners to appeal violations regardless of merit and ensure overdue penalties are paid promptly.

The bill will give MSHA additional powers to shut down a mine when there is a continuing threat to the health and safety of miners.

Also, recognizing that some mine operators may bide their time to retaliate against whistleblowers, the bill will ensure that underground coal miners are dismissed if the employer has just cause.

Finally, the bill will guarantee that basic protections are available in all workplaces.

Significant Shortcomings

Workers should have basic workplace protections no matter if they work in a mine extracting coal or at an oil refinery handling explosive chemicals.

In two dozen hearings over three-and-a-half years, this committee has not only examined gaps in mine safety, but also the significant shortcomings with the Occupational Safety and Health Act. . . .

For the second time in four decades, criminal and civil penalties will be increased and those penalties will be indexed to inflation.

Lastly, employers will have to fix safety problems more quickly, even pending appeal. Unlike mine safety laws, other workplaces are allowed to put off fixing many hazards found while the violation is appealed.

I would like to thank all those members of the House, Senate and the administration who have worked for weeks putting this legislation together.

In particular, I want to recognize the leadership of a United States Senator Robert Byrd who has been one of the coal miner's best allies in Washington. Senator Byrd was personally involved making decisions on this bill up to the last week of his life.

Recognizing the importance of Senator Byrd's legacy to our nation's miners and workers, I intend to change the name of the legislation to the Robert C. Byrd Miner Safety and Health Act of 2010.

After the 2006 Sago and Aracoma [West Virginia] tragedies, Senator Byrd said that "if we are truly a moral nation . . . [then those] moral values must be reflected in government agencies that are charged with protecting the lives of our citizens."

I agree.

Finally, this bill responds to the promise I made to families paying the ultimate price for a job our nation depends on. That promise was to do everything in my power to prevent similar tragedies.

I believe that this bill is our best chance to fulfill the promise made to the families of Aracoma, Sago, Darby [Kentucky], Crandall Canyon [Utah] and Upper Big Branch.

| "More regulation isn't needed, just better enforcement."

More Regulation Will Not Improve the Safety of Coal Mines

Tim Huber and Sam Hananel

Tim Huber and Sam Hananel are writers for the Associated Press. In the following viewpoint, Huber and Hananel contend that regulations do not adequately protect workers from the hazards of coal mines. For instance, the authors state that recent reforms focus on keeping trapped miners alive rather than protecting them from explosions to begin with. Huber and Hananel also allege that mine operators increasingly appeal violations, which creates a huge backlog of cases and delays the punishment of repeat violators. More preventive measures against disasters and better enforcement of laws—not additional regulation—are needed, the authors insist.

As you read, consider the following questions:

1. As stated by the authors, what reforms did Congress order after the mining disaster in Sago, West Virginia?

2. What preventive measures can decrease the risks of a coal mine explosion, as described by Huber and Hananel?

3. What figures do the authors cite to support their assertion that mine operators are increasingly appealing violations?

After a 2006 West Virginia mine explosion killed a dozen miners, coal companies spent more than $1 billion on new safety measures that did nothing to save the lives of at least 25 more men under similar circumstances [in April 2010].

The problem is that the safety reforms passed into law since the Sago mine disaster were focused almost exclusively on sustaining trapped miners long enough to rescue them, not on preventing underground explosions.

The result? Victims of Monday's blast at Massey Energy Co.'s Upper Big Branch mine probably died without ever getting a chance to use any of the expensive safety gear installed at the mine.

"That argues for doing more on the preventative side," said National Mining Association lobbyist Bruce Watzman. "We need to be doing both."

After Sago, where 12 miners died after being trapped for two days following an explosion, West Virginia and then Congress pushed through reforms that ordered mines to stockpile emergency oxygen, build so-called "refuge chambers," and install sophisticated wireless communications systems and other gear.

Based on surveys of mine operators, Watzman estimates the industry has spent at least $1 billion to comply with those rules in the nation's nearly 500 coal mines.

West Virginia Gov. Joe Manchin said those changes have helped, but lawmakers never considered beefing up prevention measures and still haven't, Watzman said.

"There was really no opportunity, unfortunately," he said.

Targeting Prevention

Industry officials and regulators agree that whatever reforms result from the Upper Big Branch mine should be focused on preventing explosions and other disasters.

Kentucky lawyer and safety advocate Tony Oppegard says the agency needs to push Congress to mandate six inspections of underground mines each year, rather than four.

"I've been saying this for years, but it certainly falls on deaf ears at MSHA (the federal Mine Safety and Health Administration)," Oppegard said.

Other preventive measures could include requiring coal companies to pump out the methane gas before mining a coal deposit and conducting more accurate testing to determine the flammability of conveyer belts and other mine equipment—the most common causes of mine fires.

The National Institute for Occupational Safety and Health has discovered that modern mining equipment spits out more coal dust, which can intensify a small explosion into a deadly blast.

"You've had an ignition and there's a fireball, and if the quantity of methane is sufficient, that fireball begins to move," said Jeff Kohler, the institute's associate director for mining.

Even Massey CEO [chief executive officer] Don Blankenship, an outspoken critic of the changes since Sago, thinks lawmakers need to focus more attention on preventing explosions.

"I hope the regulation that comes out of this tragedy is different than the regulation that came out of the other tragedies," he said.

Gas Buildup

Investigators believe concentrated methane gas was behind [the April 2010] explosion in Montcoal, W.Va., as at Sago. The colorless, odorless, yet highly flammable gas presents a major

---

More Safety Laws Unmerited

Perspective is hardest to achieve after a mine tragedy, but that's often when perspective is needed most. Recall that 2008 and 2009 were two successive years of record mine safety in America. More than 86 percent of our mines operated in 2009 without a lost time accident.

In view of this record, we don't believe wholesale changes in mine safety laws are merited. MSHA [Mine Safety and Health Administration] already has authorities to address unsafe practices and shut down unsafe operations—which raise questions about the need for the additional ones being advanced.

Hal Quinn,
West Virginia Coal Institute,
October 2, 2010. www.nma.org.

---

challenge for mine operators, who rely on air sensors and ventilation equipment to control methane levels underground.

Methane detectors have been commonplace in underground mines since the 1970s, but it's not clear whether they were in use at Upper Big Branch at the time of the explosion. The devices often automatically shut off the equipment they're connected to if methane levels rise past 2 percent, said Scott Shearer, CEO of CSE Corp., which makes gas sensors and emergency gear for miners. The gas generally becomes combustible at 5 percent.

MSHA has repeatedly cited the Upper Big Branch mine for problems with its ventilation system, including two large fines in January [2010] for having dirty air flowing into an escapeway where fresh air should be, and an emergency air system flowing in the wrong direction.

But Massey has frequently appealed its violations, an increasingly common tactic by mine operators following the Sago deaths. Mine companies are now contesting 27 percent of the violations they face, compared with just 6 percent in 2005.

The flood of appeals has clogged an overburdened system and allowed repeat violators to delay more serious punishment. As long as the citations are being contested, MSHA does not consider them in deciding whether there is a serious enough pattern of misconduct to warrant greater scrutiny.

Critics say the agency has been too slow to respond to these tactics and that reining in the appeals process would go a long way toward preventing catastrophes.

Celeste Monforton, an assistant professor of environmental and occupational health at George Washington University, said the [Barack] Obama administration was aware [in 2009] that a surge in appeals of violations was creating a huge backlog of cases. She said the MSHA could have changed its policy to account for the backlog by looking at more recent patterns of violations.

"That's a huge missed opportunity for the new administration," said Monforton, who spent six years as a special assistant to MSHA's assistant director.

According to an MSHA report prepared for Democratic Sen. Robert Byrd of West Virginia, the Upper Big Branch Mine met all the criteria for a pattern of violations as far back as 2007. But the mine avoided stiffer penalties, such as shutting down the mine, by reducing its rate of the most serious violations. It was unclear how.

The agency also told Byrd's office it had issued 61 orders to withdraw miners from the facility during 2009 and 2010, although it was unclear what prompted those or whether they were full or partial evacuations.

Better Enforcement

Rep. Nick Rahall, the West Virginia Democrat whose district includes the Montcoal mine, has promised congressional hearings into the disaster, but he's less certain about pushing through more changes.

"I can't say it's going to lead to a new law yet until we find the cause," he said.

United Mine Workers labor union President Cecil Roberts said more regulation isn't needed, just better enforcement.

"Mine safety laws and regulations have progressed to the point where, when followed and properly enforced, they should prevent disasters like this one at Upper Big Branch from happening," Roberts said. "Clearly that was not the case here."

> "Miners are more comfortable reporting safety problems to union officials rather than management."

Union Coal Mines Are Safer

Daniel Malloy

Daniel Malloy is a Washington correspondent for the Pittsburgh Post-Gazette. *In the following viewpoint, Malloy writes that union coal miners work in better conditions and have more leverage to address safety concerns. For instance, unions can pull miners out of dangerous mines without penalty and use safety committees to act as a mediator with management, keep miners informed of violations and other issues, and directly report miners' problems to the Mine Safety and Health Administration. As a result, union mines account for only a small percentage of fatalities, Malloy contends.*

As you read, consider the following questions:

1. According to the author, what happened to Scott Howard when he reported a large slipping rock to the mine's owner?

2. What statistics does Malloy provide corroborating his claim that union mines are safer?

3. As stated by Phil Smith, cited by the author, why has union membership declined?

Deep in a coal mine in Harlan County, Ky., one day in the late 1980s, a large rock began to slip and appeared to be inches away from falling on Scott Howard and his partner.

Mr. Howard refused to continue working in that area. His supervisor told him to go see the mine owner, whose response was curt.

"The next time a boss tells you to do something and you don't do it, you won't work for me anymore," Mr. Howard said the owner told him.

Had the mine been unionized, Mr. Howard could have reported the problem to a member of the union's safety committee and he would have been protected from potential retaliation. Instead, Mr. Howard filed a court action against the company, developing a reputation as a rabble-rouser that, he said, eventually cost him his job.

Former federal mine safety official Tony Oppegard said Mr. Howard's case is indicative of the circumstances faced by miners who lack access to protections from unsafe conditions and management retaliation that a union works to provide.

"In a nonunion mine, a miner is between a rock and a hard place," said Mr. Oppegard, of Lexington, Ky., now a mine safety lawyer who represents Mr. Howard, of Roxana, Ky., and other miners in lawsuits and complaints about safety.

"If you [raise a safety concern] in a nonunion mine, you're probably going to be fired or at least suspended," he said. "You can bring a federal action—a safety discrimination case. But that's time-consuming and could take a couple of years."

The April 5 [2010] explosion at the Upper Big Branch mine in West Virginia that killed 29 workers has spurred renewed interest in mine safety, with several investigations under way into the actions of mine owner Massey Energy and the efficacy of safety laws and their enforcement.

Workers at the Upper Big Branch mine are not represented by the United Mine Workers of America [UMW]. Union officials and others contend that the increased emphasis on safety standards found in union mines could have helped prevent the tragedy there. Their arguments are disputed by industry leaders, and Congress is unlikely to address the trend of declining unionization in the nation's mines as it examines and considers revisions to mine safety laws.

As evidence of superior safety, the UMW cited statistics it has compiled showing about 11 percent of U.S. coal mining fatalities since 2002—or 30 fatalities—have occurred at unionized mines. During that time, 28.6 percent of the work force at U.S mines has been unionized.

The federal Mine Safety and Health Administration [MSHA] and mining industry groups said they do not track safety statistics to reflect work force unionization.

MSHA had cited the Upper Big Branch mine for a series of violations before the deadly blast, which it has said was likely caused by a mixture of coal dust and methane.

If similar concerns about ventilation had surfaced at a unionized mine, the UMW could have withdrawn its workers without penalty for leaving their jobs, union spokesman Phil Smith said.

"If that was happening in a union mine, our members would have been out of there a long time ago, and they wouldn't have been producing any coal," Mr. Smith said. "To the extent that those are the issues and that's what's going on there, there's a tremendous difference between this not being a union mine and being a union mine."

Coal industry leaders, however, questioned the union figures because of the small sample size of fatalities and said safety is of paramount concern to mining companies.

In Pennsylvania, which has only a couple of union mines, Joseph Sbaffoni, director of the state Department of Mine

Safety in the Department of Environmental Protection, said he saw no correlation between safety problems and unionization.

"The union mines have safety committees, so they do have an extra set of eyes. So if there's something going on at the mine there might be one additional avenue that we may be aware of," Mr. Sbaffoni said. "But from our perspective, we don't see much of a difference between them."

Safety Infrastructure

Mark Segedi, the president of a UMW local in [Mine] Eighty Four [in Pennsylvania] and a former safety committee member, said the committees serve as a buffer between management and miners and a source of information.

The safety committee attends meetings with MSHA or state inspectors and management to keep workers apprised of violations and other issues with working conditions. The committee can also report problems raised by workers directly to MSHA, and committee members have the right to enter a mine at any time to check out a problem—and pull out workers if they believe conditions warrant that action.

Union officials also noted that miners are more comfortable reporting safety problems to union officials rather than management.

Mr. Howard said few of his friends will speak out when they face dangerous conditions. He said he's worked for intimidating mine operators, including one who addressed workers over a loudspeaker system in the mine to demand that they stop complaining about safety, adding: "I want coal on the belt."

Mr. Howard has been a part of a few efforts to organize at a mine, but all have faced resistance from mine owners and all have failed.

Coal Fatalities, 2002–10

Year	Underground Coal Fatalities	Surface Coal Fatalities	Combined Fatalities	Total Union Coal Fatalities	Total Union Representation
2002	17	10	27	3	31.3%
2003	17	13	30	6	30.5%
2004	17	11	28	5	28.9%
2005	16	6	22	4	27.5%
2006	39	8	47	6	25.0%
2007	24	9	33	2	24.1%
2008	15	14	29	3	23.0%
2009	8	10	18	1	na
2010	31	0	31	0	na
Totals	**184**	**81**	**265**	**30**	**28.6%**

United Mine Workers of America, Mine Safety and Health Administration. Energy Information Administration

TAKEN FROM: Dan Malloy, "Are Union Mines Safer?" *Pittsburgh Post-Gazette*, April 18, 2010.

Declining Membership

About 20 percent of coal mine workers are unionized now, according to federal labor statistics, down from more than 30 percent a decade ago and much higher rates in previous generations.

Mr. Smith, the UMW spokesman, attributed the decline in part to the fact that many new mines opened in recent years as the price of coal rose—and most opened as nonunion shops. That makes it more difficult for a union to gain a foothold.

Massey Energy, which owns the Upper Big Branch mine through a subsidiary, mounted an aggressive anti-union campaign in the 1980s; about 1 percent of its employees are represented by the UMW. The largest coal producer in Central Appalachia, Massey owns mines in West Virginia, Virginia and Kentucky.

"Massey was the beginning of the end of the United Mine Workers," said former Washington County miner and union organizer Kipp Dawson.

Chris Hamilton, of the West Virginia Coal Association, which represents the state's coal operators, attributed the recent drop in union membership to a less adversarial climate between management and workers.

"There's been ... basic management concepts and management of the work force that have kept pace with new-age managers and workers," he said.

Culture of a Company

He and Pennsylvania Coal Association president George Ellis said safety has more to do with the culture of a company and its employees than with what a union does.

"Even from a productivity standpoint—I don't want to sound callous or anything—but when you have a fatality, a mine shuts down," Mr. Ellis said. "Nobody's benefiting."

Massey has defended its safety record in the weeks after the Upper Big Branch explosion and has said it will cooperate with the investigations. After President Barack Obama last week [in April 2010] called the disaster "a failure first and foremost of management," the company responded in a statement saying "we fear the president has been misinformed about our record."

Massey maintains that its numbers of safety violations and efforts to challenge them are in line with those found elsewhere in the industry. It also noted that last year it received three "Sentinels of Safety" awards from MSHA—the most ever awarded to one company in a single year.

Congressional Scrutiny

As Congress investigates the Upper Big Branch fatalities and looks at possible new legislation, unionization is unlikely to play a major role in its deliberations. Last week, both House Education and Labor chairman George Miller, D-Calif., and Senate Health Education Labor and Pensions chairman Tom Harkin, D-Iowa, said unions were not a concern of their inquiries.

But Rep. Lynn Woolsey, D-Calif., the chair of the Education and Labor subcommittee on work force protections, said she hoped the mine disaster would help spark a union resurgence to help enforce the laws Congress writes.

At Upper Big Branch, a union "would have added some spine to [the law] and followed it up and made noise about this operation," Ms. Woolsey said.

"Maybe miners will realize that they need to organize. . . . If the workers had each other and they were stronger as a pack—and unions make that possible—then I think it would make a difference."

Mr. Smith said the UMW is making a renewed push to organize in mines, including a pair of new ones opening soon in Fayette and Greene counties. He acknowledged that when mounting a campaign, union organizers often talk about safety concerns, but he was hesitant to say Upper Big Branch would be a rallying point.

"We don't want to be using this for what could be seen as personal gain for the union and doing so over the bodies of those guys who died," Mr. Smith said.

"We want to talk about safety from a real perspective, but we also want to do it in a respectful way to those who lost their lives."

> *"The most important factor that enables ... companies to brutally exploit coal miners is the role of the United Mine Workers union."*

A Major Union Has Set Back Coal Mine Safety

Jerry White

Jerry White is a former presidential candidate for the Socialist Equality Party and contributor to the World Socialist Web Site. In the following viewpoint, White accuses the United Mine Workers Union of America (UMWA) of betraying its own members during a key strike in the 1980s, rolling back safety conditions in coal mines, and reducing the quality of life and rights of miners. According to White, UMWA struck selectively—not unionwide at all coal mines—leaving strikers without jobs, blacklisted, or working with strikebreakers. In fact, he claims, UMWA's actions led to a wave of frame-ups and murders of dissenting miners, violent busting of unions, and the current exploitation of workers.

As you read, consider the following questions:

1. What is the track record of violations at Massey Energy's Upper Big Branch Mine, as told by White?

2. Why was Hayes West murdered, in the author's view?

3. What is the only way coal mines can be made safer, in White's opinion?

Massey Energy—which owns the Upper Big Branch Mine in Montcoal, West Virginia, where at least 25 miners lost their lives in a methane explosion Monday afternoon [April 5, 2010,]—has a long record of sacrificing the lives and limbs of coal miners in pursuit of profit.

The nation's fourth largest coal company, Richmond, Virginia–based Massey Energy made $104 million last year [2009], twice its 2008 profits, despite continued weak demand for coal. The profits were largely gained through a vicious cost-cutting campaign, including the elimination of 700 jobs, shutting down of higher-cost mines and "significant wage and benefit reductions," according to a report on the NASDAQ web site.

At the same time, the company told investors it anticipated increasing production to 50 million tons and would increase profits by exporting more metallurgical coal to Asian steelmakers who were recovering faster than their European and US counterparts. Thus the company intends to increase production and profits with fewer workers. These workers will be driven to produce even more, while safety regulations are largely disregarded.

Last year alone [in 2009], the Mine Safety and Health Administration (MSHA) cited the Upper Big Branch Mine for 495 violations. During the same time production was tripled at the mine. Since 2005, the mine was cited for a total of 1,342 violations, including 50 in March [2010]. Asked if the mine had an unusually high rate of safety problems, Massey

CEO [chief executive officer] Don Blankenship told a West Virginia radio station Tuesday that safety violations were "a normal part of the mining process," adding that there are "violations at every coal mine in America."

Monday's disaster—with the worst US mine death toll since 1984—is only the latest in a series of fatalities at Massey operations. In 2006 a fire at Massey-owned Aracoma Alma No. 1 Mine in Logan County, West Virginia, killed two workers, Don I. Bragg, 33, and Ellery Elvis Hatfield, 47. Massey's subsidiary agreed to plead guilty to 10 criminal charges, including one felony of falsifying safety records, and to pay $4.2 million in fines, the largest ever levied in a mine fatality case.

On January 15, 2009, the *Charleston Gazette* reported that Aracoma widows Delorice Bragg and Freda Hatfield urged US District Judge John T. Copenhaver to reject Massey's plea bargain and fine for the accident, with Bragg saying it was clear "that Massey executives much farther up the line expected the Alma Mine to emphasize production over the safety of the coal miners inside." Despite their pleas, government prosecutors agreed not to bring additional charges against Massey Energy or any of its executives.

Late last year, Massey signed a letter of agreement with Blankenship, guaranteeing the CEO a base salary in 2010 and 2011 of $83,333 per month, plus a target cash incentive bonus award for each year of $1,500,000, and millions more in performance-based stock incentives. While compensation figures are not yet available for 2009, Blankenship made nearly $24 million in 2007 and $11.2 million in 2008. Earlier this year, he cashed in 200,000 shares of stock options—whose value had more than doubled, and pocketed $3.8 million.

Massey is literally able to get away with murder because it has friends in high places. In 2002, former president George [W.] Bush named former Massey Energy official Stanley Suboleski to the MSHA review commission that decides all legal matters under the Federal Mine Act. West Virginia's Supreme

Court justices have also received millions in campaign contributions, one even going along with Blankenship on a French Riviera vacation.

The United Mine Workers of America

While the company is notorious for buying politicians and judges, the most important factor that enables Massey and other companies to brutally exploit coal miners is the role of the United Mine Workers union (UMWA).

The UMWA established roots in southern West Virginia during the bitter Mine Wars of the 1920s and 1930s. Today, it represents only a small number of active miners in West Virginia, Kentucky and other Appalachian states. All told, the active membership of the UMWA has plummeted from over 120,000 in 1978 to 14,152 at present.

The struggles of coal miners led to a major increase in living standards, health care and other improvements. Today only Mississippi is poorer than West Virginia. Some of the most impoverished counties include McDowell and Mingo, two former strongholds of the UMWA.

The UMWA betrayal of the 1984–85 strike at what was then known as AT Massey set the stage for a drastic rollback in the working conditions and living standards of coal miners throughout the industry.

In September 1984, Massey refused to sign the Bituminous Coal Operators Association [BCOA] agreement—which set the standard for wages and benefits throughout the industry—and insisted that the UMWA bargain separately with 14 different subsidiaries, maintaining the legal fiction that these were independent enterprises.

Historically coal miners would carry out a national strike and shut down the entire industry until every operator signed the BCOA agreement—following the principle that "an injury to one is an injury to all." In December 1983, however, newly elected UMWA president Richard Trumka (now the head of the AFL-CIO [American Federation of Labor and Congress of Industrial Organizations]), and the rest of the union leadership abandoned the principle of "no contract, no work" and industry-wide strikes in favor of the policy of so-called selective strikes against individual companies.

In October 1984, 2,600 Massey miners struck company operations in Pennsylvania, Kentucky and West Virginia. After languishing on the picket line for nearly five months, the strike erupted into a full-scale battle with company thugs and state police in February 1985. President [Ronald] Reagan, like his British counterpart [prime minister] Margaret Thatcher, saw taking on and defeating the miners—long the most militant section of the working class—as crucial for imposing a permanent reduction in the living standards of the working class as a whole.

Massey, then controlled by giant multinational conglomerates including Royal Dutch/Shell, hired a private army of paramilitary mercenaries and used armored personnel carriers and helicopters for its strikebreaking operations, while Democratic and Republican state governments and judges in the coal states sent state police to escort scabs through the miners' picket lines and issued injunctions against the miners.

The center of the struggle was in Lobata, West Virginia, across the Tug River from eastern Kentucky and near the town of Matewan, where miners had fought hired gunmen during the Mine Wars of the 1920s. A contemporary account of the event, written in the *Bulletin*, the newspaper of the Workers League (forerunner of the Socialist Equality Party), cited the comments of Massey miner Bobby Thornsbury. "This is the story here," he said, pointing to the company thugs. "They have 70 armed guards in here and they are taking union members' jobs. The men and women in the community are fed up with it. There have been incidents where armed guards go on people's property with weapons and video equipment.

"The company has vicious attack dogs, helicopters that hover 20 feet over people's houses, and we saw 15–20 guards with guns on that road on the hill the other day. This is something you would see in another country."

Another Massey miner from Kentucky added, "Massey and the president want to break this union. AT Massey wants to take 700 men and put them on the street and hire 700 scabs to take our place. If Massey gets away with this, they will all try it."

In the face of this assault, Trumka maintained the isolation of the AT Massey strikers, refusing to mobilize the strength of more than 100,000 working UWMA miners throughout the coalfields. Instead, he ordered the miners to participate in fruitless civil disobedience stunts. Finally, after months of capitulating to the government's strikebreaking operations, Trumka called off the strike on December 16, 1985.

Hundreds of miners were left fired and blacklisted while others were forced to return on the company's terms and to work side by side with strikebreakers.

Framed Up

During the strike, on May 29, 1985, a scab coal truck driver named Hayes West was shot to death outside of Canada, Kentucky. The circumstances of the shooting indicate that it was a provocation staged by the company or its hired gunmen in order to brand the strikers as terrorists and create the pretext for the government to ban all pickcting.

Five AT Massey miners were framed up for the shooting death of West in a government effort to railroad a group of militant miners into long jail sentences and thereby intimidate the rank and file. The miners were UMWA Local 2496 President Donnie Thornsbury, David Thornsbury, Arnold Heightland, James Darryl Smith and Paul Smith.

The case, based entirely on the testimony of paid informants and stool pigeons, alleged that the shots that killed

West were fired from the top of a nearby mountain. But West was killed by a blast from a shotgun, a close range weapon, and fatally wounded by ammunition that was generally available only to police and security companies. Witnesses reported seeing guards on the mountain at the time. None testified to seeing any union miners there.

The key to the success of the frame-up was the complicity of the UMWA and its president Richard Trumka, who refused to defend the embattled miners. The union magazine, the *UMWA Journal*, never carried an article on the arrest, trial, conviction or jailing of the miners. The union provided no financial or legal assistance to the miners or their families.

With the complicity of the UMWA, the Reagan administration prosecuted and jailed four of the miners in a 1987 trial, and sentenced them to prison terms ranging from 35 to 45 years. The fifth miner, Paul Smith, was acquitted on federal charges and immediately re-arrested on state murder charges.

After serving 20 years, James Darryl Smith, 57, and David Russell Thornsbury, 55, were released in November and December 2007 respectively. Arnold Ray Heightland, 68, was released in June 2009. Donnie Thornsbury, 57, remains at a federal correctional facility in Nashville, Tennessee, with a projected release date of September 20, 2010.

These miners spent decades in jail for no other crime than fighting to defend the jobs and livelihoods of miners. In contrast, the owners and top management of Massey have never spent a day in jail for the disregard of the most elemental safety precautions that have led to the deaths of scores of miners.

A Record of Betrayal

The betrayal of the AT Massey strike by the UMWA set the stage for a wave of violent, union-busting frame-ups and the murders of militant miners over the next decade. Time and time again, from the 1989 Pittston strike, to the frame-up of the Milburn miners, to the 1990 murder of former AT Massey miner John McCoy, to the 1994 frame-up of striker Jerry Dale Lowe, the pattern was the same—the UMWA left its members defenseless and collaborated with management and the state authorities against them.

From the outset, Trumka and other UMWA leaders, including current president Cecil Roberts, sought to defend their "partnership" with the coal companies and alliance with the Democratic Party. They set out to destroy the militant and class-conscious traditions of the miners and turn the UMWA into an adjunct of management. Trumka's reward for imposing the dictates of management was to be elevated to the presidency of the AFL-CIO.

The brutal conditions of exploitation—and the horrible loss of life seen in the West Virginia mine disaster—cannot be understood outside of this record of betrayal. Overcoming these conditions is only possible on the basis of building a new organization of miners, reviving the powerful traditions of class solidarity and developing a new socialist strategy that places the needs of the working class—including safe and secure employment—above the profit interests of the wealthy few.

Periodical Bibliography

The following articles have been selected to supplement the diverse views presented in this chapter.

Adele Abrams	"Mine Disaster Will Lead to Heightened Enforcement," *Rock Products*, May 2010.
Mark Caramanica	"Data Mining in the Dark: Journalists Fight to Monitor Investigation into Recent Fatal Explosion," *News Media & the Law*, Spring 2010.
Simon Elegant and Zhang Jiachang	"Where the Coal Is Stained with Blood," *Time*, March 2, 2007.
Phil La Duke	"Are You Really Ready for World-Class Safety?" *Industrial Safety & Hygiene News*, October 2010.
Marianne Lavelle	"Mine Tragedy Amid Push to Produce More," *National Geographic News*, April 15, 2010.
Chris Lo	"Is the U.S. Falling Behind on Mine Safety?," www.mining-technology.com, June 30, 2010.
Christopher Maag	"The Real Price of Coal Mining: Investigative Report," *Popular Mechanics*, August 23, 2010.
Joe Napsha	"Mine Safety Technology on Rise in Region," *Pittsburgh Tribune-Review*, December 6, 2007.
Newsweek	"Mining and Fines Go Hand in Hand," April 7, 2010.
Michel Petrou	"Voices from the Underground," *Maclean's*, October 11, 2010.
Katherine Torres	"Breathing Easy: Respiratory Protection in Coal Mines," *Occupational Hazards*, March 2006.

For Further Discussion

Chapter 1

1. The National Energy Technology Laboratory insists that global coal consumption and its energy share are rising, therefore clean-coal technologies must be developed. In opposition of such development, Richard Heinberg states that coal quality will deteriorate in the future. In your opinion, who makes the more compelling argument? Cite examples from the texts to support your response.

2. Jude Clemente and Patrick Moore allude to terrorist attacks in their opposing arguments about the security of coal and nuclear energy. In your view, which author uses terrorism most effectively as an example? Explain your answer.

Chapter 2

1. Michael Kanellos maintains that despite renewable-energy development, coal will remain a necessity for the world's energy needs. Do you agree or disagree with Kanellos? Use examples from the viewpoints to explain your answer.

2. In your opinion, does PRWeb Newswire successfully counter the Coal-to-Liquids Coalition's claim that liquid coal is a cleaner fuel than oil? Why or why not?

Chapter 3

1. In your opinion, do Jackie Grom and Jeffrey Rubin provide convincing research that a ban on new coal-power plants will not reduce carbon emissions? Why or why not?

2. Alan H. Lockwood, Kristen Welker-Hood, Molly Rauch, and Barbara Gottlieb argue that coal power plants threaten human life with the consequences of global

warming. Paul K. Driessen maintains that a lack of electricity is responsible for diseases and suffering in developing countries. In your view, who offers the more persuasive case? Use examples from the texts to support your response.

3. Rosalind Peterson upholds that the dangers of compact fluorescent bulbs and the pollution of producing them negate the energy savings. Do you agree or disagree with the author? Why or why not?

Chapter 4

1. George Miller calls for increased legislation to crack down on operators of unsafe coal mines. On the other hand, Tim Huber and Sam Hananel allege that calling for more regulation is misguided and that focus should fall on protecting workers from explosions, not on sustaining trapped miners. In your opinion, which is the more pressing issue? Cite examples from the viewpoints to explain your answer.

2. Jerry White charges the United Mine Workers (UMW) union with the exploitation and intimidation of miners. Does White's allegation undermine the safety record of UMW mines described by Daniel Malloy? Why or why not?

Organizations to Contact

The editors have compiled the following list of organizations concerned with the issues debated in this book. The descriptions are derived from materials provided by the organizations. All have publications or information available for interested readers. The list was compiled on the date of publication of the present volume; the information provided here may change. Be aware that many organizations take several weeks or longer to respond to inquiries, so allow as much time as possible.

American Coal Ash Association (ACAA)
15200 E. Girard Ave., Suite 3050, Aurora, CO   80014-3955
(720) 870-7897 • fax: (720) 870-7889
e-mail: info@acaa-usa.org
website: www.acaa-usa.org

The ACAA is a nonprofit organization that promotes reuse of coal combustion products (CCPs), the residue left over from burning coal in a boiler. CCPs can be reused as substitutes for natural or manufactured materials in a variety of commercial applications and products. ACAA publishes *ASH at Work* magazine, containing a variety of articles on CCPs, which can be downloaded from the ACAA website.

American Coal Council (ACC)
1101 Pennsylvania Ave. NW, Suite 60
Washington, DC   20004
(202) 756-4540 • fax: (202) 756-7323
e-mail: info@americancoalcouncil.org
website: www.americancoalcouncil.org

The ACC is a private trade industry group organized to promote the development and use of American coal to enhance economic and energy security through an environmentally sound policy. The ACC promotes a nonadversarial approach to partnering coal businesses that mine, sell, trade, transport, market, or utilize coal, providing educational and technical support in a peer-to-peer atmosphere. The ACC publishes *American Coal Magazine*, fact sheets on the coal industry, *Industry Case Studies*, and the *American Coal Advisory eNewsletter*.

American Coal Foundation (ACF)
101 Constitution Ave. NW, Suite 525 East
Washington, DC 20001-2133
(202) 463-9785 • fax: (202) 463-9786
e-mail: info@teachcoal.org
website: www.teachcoal.org

The ACF is a nonprofit, nonlobbying organization designed to develop, produce, and circulate coal-related educational information and programs designed for students and teachers. The ACF has been supported at various times by coal producers, mining suppliers and equipment manufacturers, electric utilities, railroads, and unions. The foundation's website contains articles such as "Coal's Past, Present, and Future," and "Coal's Journey."

American Geological Institute (AGI)
4220 King St., Alexandria, VA 22302-1502
(703) 379-2480 • fax: (702) 379-7563
website: www.agiweb.org

The AGI is a nonprofit organization dedicated to serving the geoscience community of geologists, geophysicists, and earth and environmental scientists. It provides outreach and educational services, while striving to help the general public understand the crucial role geosciences play in the utilization of earth resources and its interaction with the environment. Publications include short books such as *Coal and the Environment*.

Citizens Coal Council (CCC)
PO Box 964, Washington, PA 15301

(724) 222-5602 • fax: (724) 222-5609
website: www.citizenscoalcouncil.org

The CCC is composed of grassroots environmental groups and individuals working to promote environmental and social justice. Its aim is to protect people, homes, communities, land, and water from coal industry operations and to enforce the Surface Mining Control and Reclamation Act, the law coal companies are meant to adhere to during and after mining operations. The CCC website contains fact sheets and studies.

Greenpeace
702 H St. NW, Suite 300, Washington, DC   20001
(202) 462-1177
e-mail: info@wdc.greenpeace.org
website: www.greenpeace.org

An international organization dedicated to environmental protection, Greenpeace uses peaceful direct action and creative communication strategies to inform the world about issues such as animal extinction and global warming. Greenpeace is supported only by direct donations from individuals worldwide. Its website contains a variety of articles on environmental action, research, and resources.

Intergovernmental Panel on Climate Change (IPCC)
IPCC Secretariat, c/o World Meteorological Organization
7 bis Avenue de la Paix, C.P. 2300, Geneva 2   CH-1211
   Switzerland
+41-22-730-8208/84/54 • fax: +41-22-730-8025/13
e-mail: ipcc-sec@wmo.int
website: www.ipcc.ch

The IPCC is a collaborative organization made up of the World Meteorological Organization (WMO) and the United Nations Environment Programme (UNEP), created to objectively assess and understand scientific and technical information relating to global climate change and its potential impact on the earth. IPCC's website contains data profiles, press releases, speeches, and reports.

International Energy Agency (IEA) Clean Coal Centre

Gemini House, 10–18 Putney Hill, London   SW15 6AA
  United Kingdom
+44 (0)20 8780 2111 • fax: +44 (0)20 8780 1746
e-mail: mail@iea-coal.org.uk
website: www.iea-coal.org.uk

The IEA Clean Coal Centre is an organization providing unbiased data and publications on sustainable coal use worldwide to governments and the coal industry through analysis, advice, and technical assistance. The organization maintains databases on coal information and technologies and publishes the *IEA CCC Newsletter* and reports.

Kentucky Coal Association (KCA)

340 S. Broadway, Suite 100, Lexington, KY   40508-2553
(859) 233-4743 • fax: (859) 233-4745
e-mail: kca@kentuckycoal.com
website: www.kentuckycoal.org

The KCA is a nonprofit organization dedicated to helping union and nonunion surface and underground miners and industry companies reach consensual agreement on and solve the most pressing problems of the coal mining industry. Its website contains Kentucky coal-mining history and editorial articles, including "True Mine Safety Reforms Ignored," and "One View: Mining Facts and Myths."

National Mining Association (NMA)

101 Constitution Ave. NW, Suite 500 East
Washington, DC   20001
(202) 463-2600 • fax: (202) 463-2666
e-mail: webmaster@nma.org
website: www.nma.org

The NMA is a nonprofit trade association and mining advocacy organization composed of lobbyists, lawyers, and regulatory experts who consult with the mining industry to develop and promote mining industry policy. NMA publishes *Interna-*

tional Coal Review Monthly and various reports such as "CO_2: A Pollutant?" The organization also created the Coal-to-Liquids Coalition (CTLC).

Natural Resources Defense Council (NRDC)
40 W. Twentieth St., New York, NY   10011
(212) 727-2700 • fax: (212) 727-1773
e-mail: nrdcinfo@nrdc.org
website: www.nrdc.org

The NRDC is an environmental action group with 1.3 million members and online activists and 350 lawyers, scientists, and other professionals. It publishes *OnEarth* magazine with an associated blog and podcasts. The NRDC also produces documentaries and audio presentations on environmental issues, climate change, and energy.

Rocky Mountain Institute (RMI)
2317 Snowmass Creek Rd., Snowmass, CO   81654-9199
(970) 927-3851
website: www.rmi.org

The RMI's major focus is creating energy efficiencies by consulting with and transforming the energy inefficiencies of large-scale users and systems. The RMI is a nonconfrontational consultant striving to help market-oriented businesses and individuals achieve resource efficiency and maximum energy security. The RMI website contains a library of publications on coal, electricity, air pollution, and energy policy.

Sierra Club
National Headquarters, 85 Second St., 2nd Floor
San Francisco, CA   94105
(415) 977-5500 • fax: 415-977-5799
e-mail: information@sierraclub.org
website: www.sierraclub.org

Founded in 1892, the Sierra Club is the nation's oldest environmental organization, with 1.4 million members. It spearheads the Beyond Coal and Campuses Beyond Coal campaigns, and Sierra Club Productions supported the documentary *Coal Country*. Its website includes news, stories, and fact sheets on coal.

US Department of Energy (DOE)

1000 Independence Ave. SW, Washington, DC   20585
(202) 586-5000 • fax: (202) 586-4403
e-mail: the.secretary@hq.doe.gov
website: www.energy.gov

The DOE is charged with fostering a safe and reliable energy system that is environmentally and economically sustainable, and with supporting scientific leadership in developing innovative energy technologies and strategies. Its Office of Fossil Energy is working with the private sector to develop innovative technologies for an emissions-free coal plant of the future. The DOE also operates the National Energy Technology Laboratory (NETL), a research and development facility.

US Department of Labor, Mine Safety and Health Administration (MSHA)

1100 Wilson Blvd., 21st Floor, Arlington, VA   22209-3939
(202) 693-9400 • fax: (202) 693-9401
website: www.msha.gov

An agency of the US Department of Labor, MSHA is responsible for mine inspections, promoting regulatory compliance with mining laws, and providing health and safety technical assistance and training to management and workers in the mining industry. MSHA's website contains numerous articles, updates, and fact sheets on the state of mining in the United States.

Bibliography of Books

Thomas G. Andrews

Killing for Coal: America's Deadliest Labor War. Cambridge: Cambridge University Press, 2008.

James T. Bartis

Producing Liquid Fuels from Coal. Santa Monica, CA: Rand, 2008.

Jeff Biggers

Reckoning at Eagle Creek: The Secret Legacy of Coal in the Heartland. New York: Nation Books, 2010.

Michael Brune

Coming Clean: Breaking America's Addiction to Oil and Coal. San Francisco: Sierra Club Books, 2010.

Shirley Stewart Burns, Mari-Lynn Evans, and Silas House, eds.

Coal Country: Rising Up Against Mountaintop Removal Mining. Berkeley, CA: Sierra Club Books/Counterpoint, 2009.

Richard J. Callahan Jr.

Work and Faith in the Kentucky Coal Fields: Subject to Dust. Bloomington: Indiana University Press, 2009.

Klaes G. Douwe

Clean Coal. Hauppauge, NY: Nova Science, 2009.

Jeff Goodell

Big Coal: The Dirty Secret Behind America's Energy Future. Boston: Houghton Mifflin, 2006.

Michael D. Guillerman

Face Boss: The Memoir of a Western Kentucky Coal Miner. Knoxville: University of Tennessee Press, 2009.

Martin Robert Karig III — *Coal Cars: The First Three Hundred Years.* Scranton, PA: University of Scranton Press, 2007.

Gerald L. McKerns — *The Black Rock That Built America: A Tribute to the Anthracite Coal Miners.* Bloomington, IN: Xlibris, 2007.

Bruce G. Miller — *Clean Coal Engineering Technology.* Burlington, MA: Butterworth-Heinemann, 2011.

Ted Nace — *Climate Hope: On the Front Lines of the Fight Against Coal.* Madison, WI: CoalSwarm, 2009.

National Academy of Sciences, National Academy of Engineering, and National Research Council — *Liquid Transportation Fuels from Coal and Biomass: Technological Status, Costs, and Environmental Impacts.* Washington, DC: National Academies Press, 2009.

Roy L. Nersesian — *Energy for the 21st Century: A Comprehensive Guide to Conventional and Alternative Sources.* Armonk, NY: M.E. Sharpe, 2010.

Joan Quigley — *The Day the Earth Caved In: An American Mining Tragedy.* New York: Random House, 2007.

David Sandalow — *Freedom from Oil: How the Next President Can End the United States' Oil Addiction.* New York: McGraw-Hill, 2008.

Michael Shnayerson — *Coal River.* New York: Farrar, Straus, and Giroux, 2008.

Brian Solomon and Patrick Yough — *Coal Trains: The History of Railroading and Coal in the United States*. Minneapolis: Voyager Press, 2009.

Gerald M. Stern — *The Buffalo Creek Disaster*. New York: Vintage Books, 2008.

Suzanne E. Tallichet — *Daughters of the Mountain: Women Coal Miners in Central Appalachia*. University Park: Pennsylvania State University Press, 2006.

Index

W

Wal-Mart, bulb replacement
movement, 139–140
"Washing," 44
Washington, CO_2 performance
standard, 111–112
Water constraints, 97
Water pollution, 44
Water removal method, 75
Watzman, Bruce, 160
Wave power, 64
Waxman-Markey climate bill, 30,
117

West, Hayes, 178–179
West Virginia mine explosion, 160
See also Upper Big Branch
mine disaster
West Virginia Office of Miners'
Health, Safety, and Training,
151–152
Whistleblowers, 156
Woolsey, Lynn, 171
Workplace protections, 156–157
See also Unionization; United
Mine Workers of America
(UMW)
World Coal Association, 19

DISCARD